Dinner Dates

Dinner Dates

A Cookbook for
Couples Cooking Together

Martha Cotton

AVON BOOKS NEW YORK

AVON BOOKS, INC.
1350 Avenue of the Americas
New York, New York 10019

Copyright © 1999 by Martha Cotton

Cover illustration by Nina Berkson
Interior design by Richard Oriolo
Inside back cover author photograph by Lance Pressl

Published by arrangement with the author
Visit our website at http://www.AvonBooks.com
ISBN: 0-380-79881-6

Library of Congress Cataloging in Publication Data:
Cotton, Martha.
    Dinner dates : a cookbook for couples cooking together / Martha
Cotton
        p.   cm.
    1. Cookery for two.   2. Dinners and dining.   I. Title.
TX652.C755   1999   98-45202
641.5'61—dc21   CIP

First Avon Books Trade Paperback Printing: February 1999

AVON TRADEMARK REG. U.S. PAT. OFF. AND IN OTHER COUNTRIES,
MARCA REGISTRADA, HECHO EN U.S.A.

Printed in the U.S.A.

OPM   10 9   8   7   6   5   4   3   2   1

This book is dedicated to three people:
Lance, my partner in the kitchen, in love, and in life.
And my Mother and Father, who taught me
everything I know and love about
cooking with others.

Acknowledgments

Many people have helped in the preparation of this book. For their support, friendship, and proofreading, I would like to thank my family, my family of friends, Katie, Jessica, Helen, Vito, all the folks at E-Lab, and Vanni and Paul who saw that this book was more than just a "good idea" and helped to make it become a reality. I thank my agent, Elizabeth Sheinkman of The Elaine Markson Literary Agency, for her helpful encouragement. I thank my editor from Avon Books, Tia Maggini, for her patient guidance. Many couples, romantic or "just friends," tested my recipes, provided inspiration, and gave helpful suggestions. I owe many thanks to Ben and Nora, Emily and Kevin, Derek and Emily, Mike and Steven, Andrea and Darren (with help from George), Jean and Rob, Kris and Lo, Jerry and Sherree, John and Liz, and Lisa and Mike. May you always find joy in cooking together!

Contents

There is little doubt that people want to find meaningful ways to enhance—and sustain—their relationships, but in today's hectic and increasingly impersonal world it gets more and more difficult to find inexpensive and creative ways to enjoy the company of others. When I was a child and my parents had dinner parties, the whole family cooked together. I was making crepes before I owned my first Barbie doll. Grateful as I am for my parents' instructions in the culinary arts, I am even more grateful for their less tangible example of the bond one can create with other people while making a meal together. I have had some of my best conversations with people important to me while chopping, stirring, measuring, or slicing food. It is a happy coincidence that what follows food preparation—food consumption—also happens to be a wonderful way to bond with others. The result is an unforgettable human interaction.

Loving to cook with others is a gift I received from my parents and siblings and that I now share with my husband, Lance. It is a gift I would like to share with you.

Dinner Dates is a cookbook for couples cooking together. It consists of a series of delicious, elegant yet simple menus that take a couple step-by-step through the preparation of an entire meal, from shopping and equipping the kitchen to dividing up the tasks necessary for preparing the menu. The directions for each recipe are shared between "Chef Uno" and "Chef Due" and are choreographed so that cooking is an enjoyable joint undertaking. In fact, the menus are designed to make the preparation experience as pleasurable and exciting as the dining experience. Why go out to a crowded, impersonal restaurant when you can have a wonderful, romantic dinner together in your own home? At the end of a Dinner Date, instead of an expensive check, a couple can take away the memory of what they created together and what they learned about each other in the process. *Dinner Dates* is more than a cookbook; it is a guidebook to romantic entertaining at home, and a springboard to a long life of love in the kitchen!

Dinner Dates

Introduction

The first step—getting a date or cooking companion—is up to you, and I have full confidence that you can accomplish this task. Once that is done, you'll need to choose your Dinner Date menu. All the recipes are designed for any skill level so even a novice chef can cook and have fun while cooking. Remember, you and your date will be cooking together, so the pressure isn't entirely on you.

Try to read the entire menu and complete instructions for the Dinner Date you are planning before you begin, so you have a good idea of what is involved and where you are headed. Make sure you read at least the Dinner Date Hints closely before you shop for groceries. As host or hostess, you should do the shopping (even if your date is with someone you already live with) and make sure your kitchen is equipped for the meal you will prepare. Both shopping and equipment lists are provided.

Look around your kitchen and think about two people cooking in that space. Is there anything you can do to make sure you have sufficient room for both of you (like putting away your toaster)? Even if you live in a tiny one-room studio with a kitchenette, two people can cook together; you just have to plan ahead a little bit. If counter space is limited, where can a second person chop? Set a cutting board on your dining table, if necessary. You'll find a way to improvise.

Depending on which menu you pick, you may have some prep work to do as the host or hostess of your Dinner Date. This will be detailed in the Host Prep section. Make sure you schedule time to do this in advance. You don't want to be rushed in the minutes before your date joins you in the kitchen.

Use the section titled Marinating the Chefs at your own whim. The term is a joke I used to have with my former roommates when we'd have big dinner parties. Marinating the Chefs was an opportunity to get the party started long before our guests arrived. Think of it as having a cocktail before your meal, as many people do in a restaurant. When possible, I try to provide nonalcoholic suggestions, so don't feel obligated to serve alcohol. Also, you may want to consider having a few munchies available: olives, carrot or celery sticks, pita wedges. You don't want to starve while you're cooking, but you also don't want to fill up either, so munch wisely!

You will see that the directions for each Dinner Date are divided into two columns. The left column details Chef Uno's tasks, and the right column details Chef Due's. You and your date will need to pick who will be Chef Uno and who will be Chef Due. You may decide this ahead of time, but remember that Chef Uno and Chef Due share all the tasks, and neither role is designed to be more difficult than the other. Each chef should proceed with his or her role following the steps assigned in the order they appear. It is a good idea for each chef to read through his or her instructions before you begin cooking. This way you'll each have a sense of the "flow" of your Dinner Date.

Make sure you tell each other periodically what you're working on. I try to build in reminders for each of you to communicate with the other. Anytime you see this icon 🍴, take a moment to talk to each other. However, if you find yourselves in the midst of a fascinating discussion about her childhood in Norway or about his choice to drop out of school and raise llamas on a farm in Wisconsin, don't be afraid to interject: "Oh by the way, I'm working on the salad now, and I'll need that lettuce you just washed."

As your date progresses, don't get too bogged down in the timing of all the dishes. If, for example, you get to a step where your date needs the onions you are chopping and you are nowhere near done, don't sweat it. Or, if you find you are standing around while your date feverishly stirs risotto, lend a hand, move on to your next step, or perhaps set the table. Again, make sure you communicate with each other while cooking: How is Chef Uno doing? What is Chef Due doing? Do you need help? Can I rub your shoulders? Can I pour you more wine? The rule is, there are no rules except to have fun, talk to each other, and enjoy the process of cooking together. If you follow that rule, everything will turn out wonderfully!

A special note to "serious" couples (i.e., you married folk, those living together, or those who have been dating a really, really, really long time), try to treat the Dinner Date as a *date*. You may go so far as to send an invitation to your significant other. Remember what it was like when you were first dating and how exciting it was? Go back to that time and stay in that special place for the whole night. You may even get butterflies in your stomach.

Atmosphere

Making your Dinner Date a truly magical one depends on several things. Don't worry about the food, it will be fabulous; but there are some other things you can do to make the date romantic and memorable.

Candlelight

Think "romantic dinner" and what is the first thing that comes to mind? Candles, of course; everyone knows that. Arrange candles all around the table, or if you are short on candlestick holders, you can buy some inexpensive votive candles and put them on little plates. Try to make your meal entirely candlelit if possible. If you want to try something different, string Christmas lights around the room (you can do this any time of year). You don't want to overdo this effect, so do it sparingly.

The Table

You shouldn't feel that you have to go out and buy new dishes and napkins, but do use your best things. Unless you need the table as a food prep area, try to set it before your date arrives, so that he or she can have a preview of what is to come. Depending on the season, decorate the table with flowers, fall foliage, or evergreen sprigs. If you have a hunch your date will bring you flowers (and I certainly hope he or she does!), keep a nice vase aside to make an instant centerpiece.

Music

Everyone has his or her own notion of romantic music. You may want to think ahead of some upbeat music to play while you're cooking and some soothing and calm music for while you're eating. Here are a few suggestions in the soothing, calm, romantic category:

- Anything featuring the Three Tenors (together or separately)
- Rachmaninoff's Second Piano Concerto (it gets a little rowdy at times, but for the most part it is incredibly romantic)
- Chopin piano music
- Beethoven piano music
- Vivaldi guitar music
- Fauré's Requiem
- Prefabricated collections of "romantic music" (they may be cheesy, but they usually have some good tunes on them)
- Anything from Frank Sinatra (of course)

Presentation

My mother raised me to think that a plate was not ready to be presented until it had some color on it. I think this was a sneaky way to get me to eat vegetables, but the lesson has stuck with me. I've tried to assemble menus that will not only taste good together, but look good together as well. However, there are some simple things you can do to enhance the presentation of food on the plate during your Dinner Date. A sprig of parsley, rosemary, or thyme, delicately placed, goes a long way to brighten up a rice or potato dish. There are also edible flowers—less popular now than a few years ago—that add beautiful color. I like to complement an overly green and yellow plate with a touch of red: sliced cherry tomatoes or red pepper will do the trick. Try dusting grated Parmesan cheese or chopped green onion around the entire plate. Also remember to arrange the foods themselves in an attractive way.

The idea is to paint a picture with the food that provides edible decoration. Simple additions can enhance the look of a meal without detracting from the taste. Be creative, awake your inner Michelangelo, and have fun!

Equipping and Stocking Your Kitchen

Equipping

When a more unusual piece of kitchen equipment is required for the preparation of a specific Dinner Date, I try to detail that in the section titled Equipment List. There are some things, however, that I assume a functional kitchen should have:

- Two or three sharp knives
- Two or three chopping boards
- At least one large and one small pot with lids
- At least one large frying pan
- At least one large and one small mixing bowl
- A cookie sheet
- A colander
- A variety of measuring spoons and cups
- One or two wooden spoons
- A wire whisk
- A timer
- A garlic press
- A pepper mill
- Wax paper
- Aluminum foil
- Microwave oven

Stocking

In the Shopping Lists for each menu, you'll notice that I list what I consider to be staples. If you are an experienced cook, you probably have your own list of things you always have on hand in the kitchen. If you are more of a beginner, you will find that as your skills develop you'll begin your own personal—and ever evolving—list of "must haves." What I list below are just those items that Lance and I always have on hand and cook with regularly. I'll list them here for you, but you may find they don't quite become staples in your kitchen.

Universal staples

- milk
- butter
- flour
- sugar
- salt
- eggs

Very good things to have

- peppercorns in a pepper mill
- balsamic vinegar
- red wine vinegar
- Dijon mustard
- fresh garlic
- soy sauce
- cooking sherry

- virgin olive oil
- yellow onions

Good dried spices to have

- oregano
- dill
- dried basil
- dried rosemary
- garlic powder
- bay leaves
- thyme
- tarragon
- sage
- cumin
- ginger
- cinnamon

Cleaning Up

When I first started talking to friends about doing this book, I was amazed that almost every single one of them, at one point or another, asked the question, Who cleans up? I suppose it follows that since you and your date created the meal together and ate it together, you should clean up together. You may find moments during the preparation of the Dinner Date to wash a dish or two, and I would encourage this to a certain degree. Regardless of how much this clean-as-you-go method is implemented, there are always a number of dishes to be washed at the end of a good meal; it is unavoidable. If you are a particularly fastidious person and cannot relax when dishes need to be done, then by all means clean up together after your Dinner Date comes to a close. However, I vote for the shut-the-door-and-forget-about-the-mess method. As long as you put away any leftovers, the dishes can wait at least until the next day. If you happen still to be together at this point, share the duties. If not, throw on some sweats, turn on some fun music, and clean up at your own pace. I hope the mess will be a sweet reminder of a fabulous date the evening before.

Your First Dinner Date

Grapefruit and Avocado Salad

Mediterranean Chicken Breasts

Green Beans with Lemon and Shallots

Basil Rice with Mushrooms

Anjou Pears Poached in Sauternes

PREPARATION TIME

About 1 hour

A little nervous because it's your first dinner date? You can relax because this menu is all about the warmth of the sun, from the Florida and California trees where grapefruit and avocado ripen, to the lush olive groves of Italy and Greece. Let the food take you to these places, and your first date will be a fabulous vacation.

Dinner Date Hints

- You need a perfectly ripe avocado. If avocados are not in season, find what you can a few days ahead and leave it on your kitchen counter to ripen. It should be soft but not mushy.

- If you are using sun-dried tomatoes packed in oil (for the Mediterranean Chicken), decrease by half the amount of oil you add to the paste. I prefer dried tomatoes that you reconstitute with hot water.

- Bosc pears can be substituted for Anjou. It is important that you purchase ripe pears. If there are no ripe pears available at your market, you may need to rethink the dessert. You could try getting a nice pear sorbet from a gourmet grocer and serving it with fresh raspberries.

- Sauternes is a delicious sweet dessert wine. It also can be a little pricey. If you'd like to keep costs low, ask the expert at your local wine store for a good, inexpensive dessert wine. They usually come in half bottles.

- You can keep the Mediterranean theme by serving a Gavi white wine. Lighter than a chardonnay, it is a specialty of the Italian Riviera.

Shopping List

Staples
Olive oil
Freshly ground pepper
Balsamic vinegar
Fresh garlic
Dijon mustard
Vanilla extract

Produce
1 yellow or pink grapefruit
1 ripe avocado
1 bunch fresh basil
1 pound green beans
2 shallots
4–5 white button mushrooms
4–5 shiitake mushrooms
1 unbruised, ripe Anjou pear
1 lemon
1 yellow onion

Dairy and Meat
2 boneless, skinless chicken breasts

Other
1 small package sun-dried tomatoes
1 baguette
White wine (see Dinner Date Hints)
Sauternes
Vanilla ice cream or vanilla yogurt
   (optional)
Long-grain rice
2 cans chicken broth
Black olives
Pine nuts
Asti Spumante (optional, see Mari-
   nating the Chefs)

Equipment List
Food processor or blender
Steamer basket

Host Prep
There is really nothing to do ahead of time foodwise, so use that time to set a spectacular table, and select some music appropriate to the culinary journey you and your date will be taking. Some Italian opera arias perhaps, or a little Vivaldi guitar music?

Marinating the Chefs

Why not celebrate the beginning of your dinner date with a glass of Asti Spumante? Bon Voyage!

Mediterranean Chicken

½ cup pitted black olives

1 tablespoon pine nuts

1–2 tablespoons olive oil

¼ cup reconstituted sun-dried tomatoes

2 boneless, skinless chicken breasts

Basil Rice with Mushrooms

½ yellow onion

4–5 white button mushrooms

4–5 shiitake mushrooms

8–10 leaves fresh basil

1 tablespoon olive oil

1 cup long-grain rice

2 cups chicken broth

1 tablespoon pine nuts

Green Beans with Lemon and Shallots

1 pound green beans

2 shallots

½ lemon

Grapefruit and Avocado Salad

1 yellow or pink grapefruit

1 ripe avocado

Olive oil

Balsamic vinegar

Dijon mustard

Salt and pepper

Anjou Pears Poached in Sauternes

1 Anjou pear

1 half bottle Sauternes

1 teaspoon vanilla

Vanilla ice cream or yogurt (optional)

1. Preheat the oven to 400°F for the chicken.

2. To make the paste for the chicken, place olives, pine nuts, and olive oil in the bowl of your food processor or blender. Wait for the sun-dried tomatoes to soften (Chef Due has this under control), then add. Process in food processor or blender until you have a thick paste. Add more olive oil if it is too thick.

3. Wash and pat dry the chicken breasts. Cover each breast on both sides with the paste and set aside. Don't forget to wash your hands after you're done handling the chicken!

4. Wash and snap the stems off the green beans. Place in the steamer basket. Don't cook them yet!

5. Finely chop the shallots for the green beans. Set aside.

6. Squeeze the juice of the half lemon and reserve.

7. Cut the avocado (with skin on) in half and remove the pit. Holding an avocado half in one hand, gently make lengthwise slices, then scoop

1. If you are using dry sun-dried tomatoes (which is what I prefer), place them in a bowl and pour boiling water over them. Set aside to soften (3 to 5 minutes).

2. For the rice, finely chop the onion and set aside.

3. Clean and then coarsely chop the mushrooms. Set aside.

4. Clean and coarsely chop the fresh basil and guess what? Set this aside too.

5. In a small sauté pan, heat the olive oil (for the rice), then add the onion and sauté. When the onion is translucent, add the mushrooms and sauté until soft. Remove from the heat and set aside.

6. Using a sharp knife, remove the skin and white part of the grapefruit. Cut out the sections of the grapefruit and arrange on two salad plates.

7. Combine ½ cup olive oil with ¼ cup Balsamic vinegar and 1 tablespoon mustard. (You can increase these amounts if you want to make more dressing, just keep the ratio of oil to vinegar, 2 to 1.) Add salt and pepper to taste.

8. When Chef Uno gives you the avocado slices, arrange them with the grapefruit on the salad plates.

out the slices with a spoon. Pass the avocado slices over to Chef Due, who will arrange them attractively on a plate.

8. Peel the pear, slice in half, and, using a spoon, scoop out the seeds. Place the pear halves in a saucepan and cover with the Sauternes. Add vanilla. Don't cook them yet!

9. Put the chicken in a roasting pan and place in the oven. Sit down to enjoy your avocado and grapefruit salad. You will need to check the chicken in 15 to 20 minutes. It is done when the meat is white all the way through and the juices run clear when poked with a knife.

10. Enjoy being together, and take your time with the salad course.

11. About 5 minutes before the chicken is done, turn on the heat under the beans and steam until just tender. In a serving dish, toss while still warm with the shallots and lemon juice.

12. Just before you sit down to the chicken, turn the heat on high under the pears. Check in 5 minutes or so and, if the wine is boiling, reduce heat to low. They should be done in about 30 minutes. You'll want them to be tender all the way through.

9. Drizzle the dressing on the salad. Put the salad plates on the table.

10. Back to the rice: Place rice (1 cup) and broth (2 cups) in a saucepan over high heat. When it boils, reduce heat to simmer and cover the pot. You will need to check the rice in about 25 minutes.

11. Open the wine (if you haven't already).

12. Wrap the baguette in tin foil and put it in the oven when the chicken goes in.

13. When Chef Uno gets up to check the chicken, see how the rice is doing. You want all the liquid to be absorbed.

14. When the rice is ready, stir in your mushroom sauté with the rice. Then quickly stir in the fresh basil and pine nuts. Reheat slightly if necessary. Put in a serving dish and bring out to the table with the chicken. Don't forget to grab the bread out of the oven!

15. SALUT!

13. When done, transfer the pears to two dessert bowls but reserve the liquid. You can eat them hot or cold, so just keep them aside until you're ready for dessert. When serving, top pears with the poaching liquid and a scoop of vanilla ice cream.

14. SALUT!

A Celebration for Two

Champagne and Smoked Salmon

Leg of Lamb

Wild Mushroom Risotto

Carrot and Parsnip Money with Snow Peas

Cucumber Salad with Balsamic Vinaigrette

White Chocolate Mousse

PREPARATION TIME

Approximately 1$\frac{1}{2}$ hours
(with a break in the middle for champagne and salmon)

This menu is not only deceptively easy to prepare, it is also a romantic way to honor any celebration in your or your date's life. I have used this menu to ring in the New Year, but sometimes little celebrations make good excuses for a fabulous meal. It's Friday? Pop open some champagne and celebrate!

Dinner Date Hints

- Take your time in making this meal. The risotto is the only dish that requires more specific timing, but risotto is fun if you have someone to talk to while you stir.

- It is absolutely crucial that you buy Italian Arborio rice for the risotto. Trust me on this one. Most groceries carry it these days.

- Try to get deluxe smoked salmon sliced very thin—you may have to go to a specialty store. If this is not an option, the best Nova Lox your local deli offers will do.

- Try to get your lamb from a butcher, or an upscale grocery. It is okay to have a larger piece of lamb; it will make great leftovers.

- When I was a kid my mother tried to make vegetables more appealing by cutting carrots into the round discs and calling them money. I guess it worked since I love veggies as a grown-up.

- Use good imported white chocolate for the mousse. I like the Swiss chocolate I can find at a gourmet grocer.

- Use imported aged Parmesan cheese, and grate it directly into the risotto.

- When carving the lamb, try to make each slice as thin and elegant as possible.

- You can stick with champagne through the meal, or move to a nice French burgundy after the lamb is served.

Shopping List

Staples

Olive oil
Freshly ground pepper
Salt
Dried dill
Fresh garlic
Dijon mustard
Balsamic vinegar
Vanilla

Produce

1 ounce dried porcini mushrooms
6 shiitake mushrooms
6 crimini mushrooms
1 yellow onion
3 medium carrots
3 parsnips
1 cucumber
1/2 cup snow peas
8–10 cherry tomatoes
Fresh chives
Fresh rosemary
Fresh raspberries (optional)
1 bunch parsley

Dairy and Meat

3–4 pounds leg of lamb
Milk
Butter
Eggs
1 pint whipping cream

Other

Smoked salmon (8–10 slices)
Arborio rice
2 cans chicken broth
Aged Parmesan cheese
9 ounces fine white chocolate
Brown bread, sliced thin
Champagne
Burgundy

Equipment List

Roasting pan and rack for the lamb
Meat thermometer
Double boiler (any stainless steel
    bowl that fits well into a
    saucepan)
Handheld mixer

Host Prep

If you have the time, prepare the lamb for cooking the morning of or even the night before your date. You want to allow time for the flavors to mingle with the meat.

Make the white chocolate mousse at least 2 to 3 hours before your guest arrives (or even the night before).

Leg of Lamb

3 sprigs fresh rosemary (1½ tablespoon dry)

3–5 tablespoons Dijon mustard

3–4 pounds leg of lamb

3–5 cloves garlic, thinly sliced

Salt

Pepper

1. Gently remove the rosemary leaves from the stem. In a bowl, combine the mustard and half of the rosemary. Set aside.

2. With a sharp knife, make small incisions in the lamb just big enough to insert a slice of garlic and a piece of rosemary. Work your way around the lamb, making your cuts 1 to 2 inches apart. Remember, the more garlic you use the more good garlicky taste!

3. Using a spatula or your hands, cover the lamb in the mustard mixture. Place the lamb on a plate and cover loosely with plastic wrap. Refrigerate until 1 hour before cooking.

White Chocolate Mousse

This recipe makes about four servings of mousse. You can cut the recipe in half if you don't want the extra servings, but the mousse will keep for a few days and it makes delicious leftovers. Besides, you and your date may love it so much that you eat the whole thing in one sitting!

9 ounces white chocolate, broken into pieces

$\frac{1}{3}$ cup milk

2 cups whipping cream

2 egg whites

$\frac{1}{2}$ teaspoon vanilla

Fresh raspberries for garnish (optional)

1. Place enough water in the pan of your double boiler to leave at least an inch between the water and the bottom of the bowl. Place over medium heat, and add the white chocolate to the bowl. Stir occasionally until smooth.

2. Meanwhile, heat the milk over low heat until just warm. When the milk is warm and the chocolate is melted, stir the milk into the chocolate and mix well. Remove from heat.

3. Whip the cream until very soft peaks form. Try not to overwhip! Set aside.

4. Whip the egg whites until soft peaks form. Fold the egg white into the chocolate mixture. Pour this mixture over the whipped cream, add vanilla, and fold it all together quickly. (For tips on folding, please see Helpful Hints.)

5. Spoon mousse into champagne glasses (or any glass or bowl). Refrigerate at least 2 hours.

6. Garnish with fresh raspberries before serving (optional).

The Dinner Date

Marinating the Chefs

Champagne and more champagne. Splurge, if you wish, for a bottle of really good bubbly. Make sure you've always got a bottle cold, and keep it flowing!

Carrot and Parsnip Money with Snow Peas

3 carrots, peeled

3 parsnips, peeled

$\frac{1}{2}$ cup snow peas

3 tablespoons butter

1 teaspoon dried dill

Freshly ground pepper

Risotto

$\frac{1}{2}$ ounce dried porcini mushrooms

2 cups hot water

1 yellow onion

3 crimini mushrooms

3 shiitake mushrooms

1 tablespoon olive oil

1 cup Arborio rice

3 cups chicken broth

$\frac{1}{2}$ cup Parmesan cheese

$\frac{1}{4}$ cup chopped parsley

Vinaigrette

¼ cup olive oil

2 tablespoons balsamic vinegar

1 teaspoon Dijon mustard

¼ teaspoon dill

Salt

Freshly ground pepper

Smoked Salmon

Chives

Butter

Brown bread

8–10 slices smoked salmon

Cucumber Salad

1 cucumber

8 cherry tomatoes

Chopped onion

Vinaigrette (see above)

1. Preheat oven to 350°F.

2. Place the dried porcini mushrooms in a bowl and add 2 cups hot water. Set aside.

3. Chop the onion for the risotto. Set aside.

4. Clean, trim, and chop the fresh mushrooms for the risotto. Go ahead and set these aside as well.

5. Place the lamb on a rack inside a roasting pan. Once oven is heated, roast the lamb approximately 20 minutes to the pound. Set the timer for 50 minutes to check it.

6. Rinse and chop the chives for your appetizer.

7. Spread a small amount of butter on each slice of bread.

8. Place a slice of salmon on each slice of buttered bread. Garnish each with the chives.

9. Place a paper towel inside a small colander or sieve, and place this over a larger bowl.

10. Drain the porcini mushrooms through the colander, saving the mushroom water in the bowl. Coarsely chop the porcini mushrooms.

1. Get to work slicing those carrots and parsnips. Make your slices as round and thin as possible. (If there is a food processor available, you can take a shortcut and slice the veggies using the thinnest slicing attachment. Set aside.

2. In a small bowl, mix together oil and vinegar for the vinaigrette.

3. Using a fork, whip the mustard into the oil and vinegar mixture until smooth.

4. Add dill, then salt and pepper to taste.

5. Add more mustard for more kick if desired, and give Chef Uno a taste. Set aside.

6. Back to the veggies: rinse and trim the snow peas (snap the ends off each and remove any strings from the side—think of it like opening a Band-Aid). Set aside.

7. Peel the cucumber, and slice into thin rounds.

8. Slice the tomatoes in half.

11. Relax, drink some champagne, and enjoy the smoked salmon while you wait for the timer on the lamb to ring.

12. When the timer rings, see how the lamb looks, and start the risotto. Depending on how big the leg of lamb is, you may want to start checking the internal temperature; 145°F is medium rare.

13. For the next 20 minutes you will be stirring the risotto, so get ready. Don't forget to check the lamb! If the lamb is finished before you are, don't worry. Just remove it from the oven and cover with tin foil.

14. Heat 1 tablespoon olive oil in a medium-sized saucepan. Add chopped onion and sauté until just translucent. Add the chopped mushrooms and sauté until soft. Add the Arborio rice and sauté to coat the rice.

15. Add ½ cup of the warmed broth Chef Due has so nicely prepared for you. Stir until the broth is absorbed. Continue in this fashion until all the broth has been used up.

16. Add the reserved mushroom water from the porcini mushrooms and stir this until the water is absorbed. Taste the risotto for doneness: it should be only slightly firm. Add water and stir if rice is too firm.

9. Arrange the sliced cucumber and tomatoes attractively on two salad plates. Grab a tiny amount of the onion Chef Uno chopped for the risotto (your partner won't mind), and sprinkle on the salads.

10. See Chef Uno step 11.

11. When the timer rings, put chicken broth in a small saucepan and bring to a slow simmer. Make sure the pan is near where Chef Uno will be overseeing the risotto.

12. Grate a generous ½ cup of Parmesan cheese and set aside.

13. Chop ¼ cup parsley for the risotto and set aside.

14. You can help in stirring the risotto when Chef Uno needs a break. Risotto must be stirred constantly while it cooks so the rice absorbs the liquid evenly.

15. Remember all those vegetables you chopped and set aside? When the lamb is just about done, you're ready for them. Melt the butter (3 tablespoons) in a pan (a sauté or frying pan will do).

17. Stir the grated Parmesan and chopped parsley into the risotto and add fresh ground pepper to taste.

18. When the lamb is done, put plates in the still warm oven to heat. It is a good idea to let the lamb sit under foil for 10 minutes after you remove it from the oven (it will carve more easily).

19. On a plate place a small amount of the risotto to form a bed for the lamb. Place two slices of lamb on the risotto and top with some of the lamb juices from the pan.

20. TOAST TO YOUR CELEBRATION!

16. Add the carrots, parsnips, and snow peas to the melted butter. Sauté until just soft (4 to 6 minutes).

17. Add dill and remove from heat. Cover to keep warm. The veggies can be quickly reheated by stirring over heat for one minute if they cool.

18. Add a spoonful of the veggies to each plate with lamb and risotto on it.

19. Drizzle a little of the vinaigrette on each salad plate.

20. CELEBRATE!

Everyone Loves Pasta

Green Salad with Herbed Vinaigrette

Penne with Lance's Excellent Tomato Sauce

Garlic Bread

Italian Ices

PREPARATION TIME

About ½ hour

For me these recipes fall under the category of comfort food. If you or your date has had a particularly grueling week, make this wonderfully tasty but easy menu together and unwind. Your minds and stomachs will thank you. The sauce is named for Lance because he took my simple tomato sauce and made it better.

Dinner Date Hints

- Penne is wonderful for catching sauce with its quill-like, tubular shape. If you have a different favorite pasta shape, feel free to use it.

- Plum tomatoes are the rather oblong, smallish variety. You can substitute another kind if you feel they look better than the plum tomatoes your grocer offers.

- Please, please, please use fresh Parmesan cheese. We have a hand-cranked grater that we keep in the fridge always loaded with a hunk of Parmesan. If you use a regular grater, grate the cheese fine. You won't need much because it is so flavorful.

- If possible, buy a nice loaf of Italian bread. Don't be afraid to use the garlicky slices of bread to sop up sauce as you eat.

- Try a Chianti as your red wine selection. This menu is rather low-cost, so splurge on the wine. My "uncle" Lou says fuggedaboudit if it's not a Chianti Riserve.

- You can find Italian ices in the freezer aisle at your grocery store. If you want a richer taste, try Spumoni ice cream.

Shopping List

Staples

Olive oil
Salt
Freshly ground pepper
Red wine vinegar
Fresh garlic
Dried oregano

Produce

Boston lettuce
1 cucumber
1 yellow onion
1 carrot
5 Italian plum tomatoes
8–10 white mushrooms
1 bunch fresh basil

Dairy

Butter
Fresh Parmesan cheese

Other

Italian bread
Italian ices
1 can crushed tomatoes
Penne
Red wine
1 can tomato paste
Peach nectar and champagne
   (optional, see Marinating the
   Chefs)

Equipment List

Cheese grater (see Dinner Date
   Hints)

Host Prep

None whatsoever.

The Dinner Date

Marinating the Chefs

You can open your bottle of Chianti early and have a glass, or if you're feeling adventurous, try this simple version of a Bellini, a Venetian drink made famous by Ernest Hemingway. Mix peach nectar with inexpensive champagne (proportions are up to you).

Penne with Lance's Excellent Tomato Sauce

2 cloves garlic (use more, if you like)

1 yellow onion

1 tablespoon olive oil

8–10 white mushrooms

5 Italian plum tomatoes

$^1/_2$ can crushed tomatoes (14 ounces)

$^1/_2$ can tomato paste (3 ounces)

$^1/_4$ cup butter

Fresh basil (about 2 stalks)

Salt

Freshly ground pepper

Dried oregano

Penne

Fresh Parmesan cheese

Garlic Bread

¼ cup butter

2 cloves garlic

1 loaf Italian bread

Green Salad
with Herbed Vinaigrette

Boston lettuce

½ cucumber

Olive oil

Red wine vinegar

Salt

Freshly ground pepper

Dried oregano

1. Remove 1 stick of butter from fridge to let soften for the sauce and bread. Preheat oven to 350°F (for the garlic bread).

2. Finely chop the onion.

3. Rinse and lightly scrub the mushrooms and chop the end off the stems. Slice the mushrooms.

4. Clean the tomatoes, and chop coarsely.

5. Sorry, Chef Uno, more chopping for you! Rinse the basil (start with 8 to 10 leaves), and coarsely chop. Set these aside.

6. Slice the bread, leaving a small amount uncut on the bottom crust, so that the loaf is still intact but slices are separated.

7. Place ¼ cup soft butter in a small bowl and cream slightly with a spoon. Using the garlic press, squeeze 2 cloves garlic into the butter and cream together well. You can also add some dried oregano here if you like.

8. Spread this butter mixture in between the slices of bread. Be generous! Wrap loaf with foil and place in

1. Peel all garlic cloves (for the bread and the sauce).

2. In a large sauté pan, heat the olive oil. Using a garlic press, squeeze two cloves garlic in the pan and sauté over medium heat until just golden.

3. Depending on Chef Uno's progress, add the onions at this point or lower heat until onions are ready. Sauté until translucent.

4. How is Chef Uno doing? Lend a hand chopping if necessary (turning heat down first). Add the chopped mushrooms to the onions once they are ready, and sauté until soft.

5. Add the tomatoes as Chef Uno finishes chopping them. Continue sautéing over medium heat.

6. When the tomatoes start to break down a bit and get soft, add the ½ can of crushed tomatoes and stir well. Then add the half can of tomato paste. Turn heat down and let sauce simmer.

7. Add butter, salt, pepper, and a couple of pinches of dried oregano to sauce and taste. Continue to let sauce simmer.

8. Take the most attractive leaves off the head of Boston lettuce and wash thoroughly. Break into bite-size pieces and place in a salad bowl. Take a second to stir your tomato sauce.

the oven for about 15 minutes or until the pasta is ready.

9. Place a large pot of water on the stove and turn heat to high, for the penne.

10. When the water boils, add the pasta and cook till al dente (ever-so-slightly firm), unless your preference is for softer pasta.

11. Drain the pasta and place a serving each on two plates. Add sauce on top.

12. Grate a generous portion of fresh Parmesan over each pasta plate.

13. Remove bread from oven and eat while hot.

14. Open the wine! Salut!

9. Peel the cucumber and slice thinly. Add to the salad bowl.

10. Assemble the vinaigrette ingredients, and have them ready for an at-the-table preparation.

11. Add the chopped basil to your tomato sauce and stir until it is incorporated. Continue to simmer the sauce.

12. Whenever you and your date are ready to eat the salad, prepare the dressing by pouring 1 large spoonful of olive oil over the salad bowl, followed by 2 large spoonfuls of vinegar. Add a sprinkle of salt, some twists of fresh ground pepper, and a pinch of oregano. Toss the salad until mixed, and enjoy!

13. Don't forget the Italian ices after dinner!

Fun with Fajitas

Killer Margaritas

Guacamole

White Rice and Black Beans

Chicken and Steak Fajitas

Ice-Cream Sundaes

PREPARATION TIME

About 1 hour

No, your food won't arrive on a sizzling platter, and a live mariachi band won't serenade you—though you could hire one—but you and your date will have lots of fun with your homemade fajita feast. You may never go out for a combo platter again!

Dinner Date Hints

❧ Ripe avocados are a must for the guacamole. Gently squeeze them before you make your purchase; you want them to be soft. To be on the safe side, check them out at your grocery store a few days ahead of time; you can always buy them hard and let them ripen at home.

❧ If you want the absolute best margaritas, buy top-shelf tequila and orange liqueur. I omit sugar from my recipe because it decreases the chances of a hangover, but if you and your date find them too tart, add a splash of orange juice or sour mix.

❧ Cilantro resembles parsley and can be found fresh in the produce section of your grocery store. Fresh is best, but if you cannot find it, you can use the dried version found with other spices. Cilantro is also known as coriander leaf.

❧ You can add a little more class to your fajitas by using shrimp instead of the chicken or steak. Peel, wash, and devein the shrimp and follow the recipe, substituting shrimp for chicken.

❧ Be careful to avoid what has become my downfall with Mexican food: filling up on chips and salsa before your main course arrives!

❧ Play some fun mambo music while you are cooking, and then perhaps tone it down a bit for eating with the mellower Gypsy Kings.

Staples

Olive oil
Freshly ground pepper
Salt
Cumin

Produce

4 ripe avocados
4 plum tomatoes
1 green pepper
2 yellow onions
1 head garlic
10 large limes
1–2 jalapenos
1 bunch fresh cilantro

Dairy and Meat

2 chicken breasts
1 steak
1 8-ounce container sour cream
1 brick Monterey Jack cheese
1 pint whipped cream
Ice cream (as much as you want!)

Other

1 bag tortilla chips
Your favorite salsa
Flour tortillas
White rice
1 can prepared black beans
1 packet fajita seasonings
1 can chicken broth
Chocolate syrup
Tequila
Orange liqueur
1 beer

Equipment List

Masher
Margarita glasses (optional, a wine-
    glass would work, too)
Juicer
Cheese grater

Host Prep

Nada. Do make sure you have plenty of bowls available for fajita toppings, though.

The Dinner Date

Marinating the Chefs

You'll notice that the first task for Chef Uno and Chef Due to complete is making the margaritas. Try to limit yourself to just one while you are cooking, or you may be dancing on the table before date's end. For a nonalcoholic marinade, try a lime-flavored seltzer, maybe with a splash of lime or orange juice.

Margaritas

1 cup fresh lime juice

1 cup tequila

½ cup orange liqueur

Ice

Sugar (optional)

Orange juice (optional)

Guacamole

5 ripe avocados

3 cloves garlic

½ yellow onion

1–2 jalapenos (optional)

1–2 plum tomatoes

¼ teaspoon cumin

Salt

Freshly ground pepper

Fresh lime juice

White Rice and Black Beans

1 tablespoon olive oil

½ yellow onion

2 cloves garlic

1 cup white rice

2 cups chicken broth

1 can prepared black beans

½ cup chopped fresh cilantro

Chicken and Steak Fajitas

1 tablespoon olive oil

2 chicken breasts

1 steak

1 yellow onion

1 green pepper

1 packet fajitas seasonings

Fresh lime juice

1 cup beer

Flour tortillas

Monterey Jack cheese

Chopped tomatoes

Salsa

Sour cream

Chef Numero Uno

1. Squeeze the juice out of all the limes you have (you will use some of this for the margaritas, some for the guacamole, and the rest for the fajitas).

2. Peel and mince five cloves of garlic. Three of these are for the guacamole, two are for the rice.

3. Peel two yellow onions. Chop one of the onions, you will use one half for the guacamole, the other half will be used for the rice. Slice the other onion in half, then cut into thin slices, for the fajitas.

4. You thought chopping garlic and onion was bad, get ready for the jalapenos. I recommend wearing rubber gloves and placing wax paper on your chopping board before you begin. (The jalapenos are optional; gauge your tolerance for heat, and add them only if you want some kick.) Clean and seed the jalapenos, then chop well. If you have not chopped the jalapenos while wearing gloves, wash your hands well and *watch out* if you feel the need to rub your eyes!

5. In a medium-sized saucepan, heat the olive oil.

6. Add garlic and chopped onion (from step 3) to hot olive oil. Sauté until soft.

Chef Numero Due

1. If desired, salt the rims of your margarita glasses: Run a lime half that Chef Uno has finished squeezing around the rim of each glass. Then pour salt on a plate and dip the rims of the glasses in the salt.

2. In a large pitcher, combine the tequila, orange liqueur, and lime juice (when it is ready). Stir well. Add ice to pitcher and stir again. Serve them on the rocks or straight up.

3. Cut each avocado in half and remove the pits. Scoop out the meat of each half into a medium-sized bowl. Mash together with a fork or potato masher.

4. Coarsely chop all four plum tomatoes. Two of these are for the guacamole, and the other two are to be used as a condiment and can be placed in a bowl and put aside. Add the two chopped tomatoes to the mashed avocado.

5. Add garlic and onion to the avocado and tomato mixture as they become available (Chef Uno's working on this and will tell you how much to add). Stir to mix all the ingredients.

6. Add the jalapeno and mix again. Add 1/4 teaspoon cumin, then salt, pepper, and lime juice to taste.

7. Add the rice and continue to sauté until it is well coated and turning golden brown.

8. Add the chicken broth and bring to a boil. Once boiling, reduce the heat to low, cover the pot, and set timer for 15 minutes.

9. Clean, seed, and slice the green pepper into strips.

10. Grate the Jack cheese into a bowl, and set aside.

11. Chop the cilantro (enough to yield about ½ cup). This is for the rice. Set aside.

12. Place all remaining condiments (salsa, sour cream, etc.) in bowls, and set aside.

13. Check your rice! You will want to add the black beans to the rice while there is still liquid to be absorbed (after about 15 minutes; when your timer rings). Make sure to drain liquid from canned beans. Stir well and continue to cook, covered, over low heat for about 5 more minutes, or until rice is tender.

14. When rice is done, stir in the fresh cilantro.

15. There are several ways you can heat tortillas. You can heat them in a

7. Open up a bag of tortilla chips, and you and Chef Uno can snack on the guacamole while you cook. Be careful not to fill up!

8. Slice the chicken into strips and place in a bowl. Wash your hands after handling the chicken.

9. Slice the steak into strips and place in a different bowl.

10. Sprinkle the fajitas seasonings over each bowl, dividing contents between the two. Stir well to cover the meats. Set aside.

11. In a large frying pan, heat the olive oil. Once hot, add the sliced yellow onion (chopped earlier by Chef Uno) and sauté until it is just getting soft.

12. Add the chicken and pepper strips. Stir well to brown the chicken, then add the beer and about a tablespoon of lime juice (more if you want).

13. Cook the chicken, stirring frequently until the chicken is springy when pressed with your spoon. You can also cut into a chicken strip to check for doneness.

14. Once the chicken is ready, remove from the pan and put aside. Then add

clay tortilla warmer, zap them individually in a microwave for 10 seconds each. Or place them over a gas burner and heat 5 to 10 seconds on each side. If you use the latter method, be careful not to burn your fingers! Use tongs if you have them.

16. Build the fajitas, serve some beans and rice with a little cheese sprinkled on top, and enjoy!

17. Keep making fajitas for each other. Make sure you and your date try all the condiments. When you are ready for dessert, make each other sundaes with plenty of chocolate syrup and whipped cream.

the steak, and cook until desired doneness.

15. Once the steak is ready, return the chicken to the pan and stir to reheat.

16. Build yourself a fajita with any (or all!) of the condiments. Don't forget the guacamole! Serve yourself some beans and rice with a little of the grated cheese sprinkled on top.

17. See Chef Uno step 17.

A Beautiful Birthday Dinner Date

Market Greens Salad with Walnuts, Goat Cheese, and Sun-Dried Tomatoes

Stuffed Tenderloin of Pork with Sherry Sauce

Twice-Baked Potatoes

Steamed Asparagus

Birthday Tarts with Assorted Chocolates

PREPARATION TIME

About 1 hour

Use this elegantly casual meal to celebrate any birthday. Yours, your date's, Abraham Lincoln's, it really doesn't matter. It's someone's birthday somewhere!

Dinner Date Hints

- Market greens can consist of any nice assortment of lettuce, arugula, radicchio, or endive. Go to your market's produce section and pick out anything that strikes your fancy.

- Buy a small amount of fresh goat cheese at the gourmet cheese section of your grocery store. You can substitute a more pungent Roquefort or any blue cheese if you like a little more kick.

- You should be able to buy prosciutto in the deli section of your local market. Substitute imported ham if you need to.

- You will probably have leftover twice-baked potatoes. Not to worry; they make excellent lunches during the workweek.

- Select a medium-bodied red wine to go with the pork, like a pinot noir. Ask the expert at your local wine store for a suggestion.

- You have a choice with the birthday tarts: You can make them yourself (recipe to follow), or, if you know a great bakery and don't have a lot of time, you can buy them. My thoughts? Homemade is always delicious and impressive. I've made it a little easier by suggesting pre-made pastry dough.

- Get a small but fancy assortment of gourmet chocolate. If you're feeling particularly romantic, serve Baci chocolates from Perugina. Baci means kiss in Italian, and each chocolate comes with a little love note in four languages. The possibilities are endless. . . .

Staples

Olive oil
Red wine vinegar
Garlic powder
Dijon mustard
Fresh garlic
Freshly ground pepper
Sugar*
Flour*
Vanilla*

Produce

Assorted market greens
4–5 large white mushrooms
Fresh sage (or dried)
About 1 pound asparagus
3 baking potatoes
1 yellow onion
Strawberries*
Blueberries*
1 lemon
1 kiwi*

Dairy and Meat

Milk*
Eggs*
Goat cheese
Monterey Jack cheese
Butter
1 pork tenderloin
4 slices imported prosciutto

Other

1 small package sun-dried tomatoes
Chopped walnuts
Pre-made pie shell* (I prefer fresh
    over frozen)
Assorted chocolates
Strawberry jam*
Pinot noir (see Dinner Date Hints)
Pinot grigio (see Marinating the
    Chefs)
Dry sherry

Equipment List

Roasting pan and rack
Butcher's twine or toothpicks
Potato masher
Cheese grater
Rolling pin*
Tart pans* (use small, nicely shaped
    tart pans for individual servings.
    You can find an assortment at
    kitchen speciality shops—heart-
    shaped might be nice)
Pebbles,* beans,* or anything that
    can withstand baking (for the tart
    shells)
Double boiler* (any bowl that fits
    into a saucepan)

*These items are unnecessary if you
purchase pre-made tarts

Host Prep

If you don't have a microwave, get those baking potatoes in the oven an hour before your guest arrives!

If you're preparing your own tarts, you can make the pastry cream and bake the pastry dough up to a day ahead, then assemble the tarts in the hours before your date arrives. If you had to buy frozen pie dough, be sure to give it enough time to thaw. Follow the manufacturer's directions for baking the tart shells. You want them fully cooked.

Note: The final glaze should be put on the tarts just prior to serving.

Birthday Tarts

1 pre-made pie shell

PASTRY CREAM
¾ cup milk

¼ cup sugar

2 tablespoons all-purpose flour

2 well-beaten egg yolks

Vanilla

FILLING
Assorted sliced fruits

Strawberry jam (for the glaze)

MAKING THE PASTRY CREAM

1. Scald the milk (heat to almost, but not quite, boiling).

2. Mix sugar, flour, and egg yolks on top of a double boiler, and beat until light.

3. Add the scalded milk ¼ cup at a time and stir well until all is blended.

4. Continue cooking over medium heat, stirring constantly until mixture begins to thicken.

5. Remove from heat and keep stirring until mixture is smooth and stops steaming. Add vanilla to taste.

6. Let cool before filling tarts. If you are preparing the pastry cream a day in advance, let it cool before refrigerating. You may want to stir occasionally so no skin forms on top of the cream while it is cooling. You can even cover the top of the cream with plastic wrap—this delays the cooling but prevents a skin from forming.

PREPARING THE TART SHELLS

1. Follow directions for thawing and cooking the pre-made pastry dough. Divide the rolled dough into pieces big enough to cover each tart pan generously. Drape the dough over the tart pan, then ease the dough into the pan. Cut off loose ends with a knife. Continue until all tart pans are filled. Prick each tart with a fork 5 to 6 times.

2. Before baking, line the inside of each dough-filled tart pan with foil, and place a few washed pebbles, beans, or metal chips inside the foil. This keeps the dough from bubbling or shrinking too much. Bake 7 to 10 minutes and check for doneness. Keep an eye on them; they get brown very quickly!

3. Remove from oven and let cool before lifting the shell from the pan.

ASSEMBLING THE TARTS

1. Spread a layer of cooked pastry cream in the bottom of a cooked tart shell.

2. Wash and stem the strawberries and blueberries. Slice the kiwi. You may want to slice the strawberries. Do what you think looks best.

3. Arrange the fruit attractively in the tart. Arrange the tarts on a plate. You can make all the tarts assorted fruit, or each one for one fruit only, whatever you find more aesthetically pleasing. Keep refrigerated until ½ hour before serving.

THE FINAL TOUCH

Just before serving, heat about a half of a jar of strawberry jam in a small saucepan until it is liquidy and bubbly. Spoon a little over each tart and serve.

Marinating the Chefs

Have a glass (or two) of a crisp and light pinot grigio. It will also go nicely with the salad. Keep the bottle nearby for basting the pork.

Stuffed Tenderloin of Pork

1 pork tenderloin

Freshly ground pepper

Fresh or dried sage

White wine (use the pinot grigio you are drinking)

STUFFING

4–5 large white mushrooms

½ yellow onion

1 clove garlic

1–2 tablespoons olive oil

4 slices prosciutto

Market Greens Salad

5–6 sun-dried tomatoes

Assorted market greens

Fresh goat cheese

¼ cup chopped walnuts

Freshly ground pepper

Red wine vinegar (optional)

Twice-Baked Potatoes

3 baking potatoes

½ yellow onion

1 cup Monterey Jack cheese

3 tablespoons butter

Garlic powder to taste

Salt

Freshly ground pepper

Steamed Asparagus

1 pound asparagus

Lemon wedges

Sherry Sauce

½ cup dry sherry

2 tablespoons butter

1. Preheat oven to 400°F for the pork.

2. Place the prosciutto in the freezer. (This will make it easier to slice later.)

3. Wash the potatoes and prick with a fork. Place in microwave for 10 minutes.

4. Wash and pat dry the pork tenderloin. With a sharp knife, cut a 2- to 3-inch slit lengthwise in the center of the loin. Carefully use your knife to make the inside pocket bigger than the opening.

5. Season the whole tenderloin with freshly ground pepper and sage. If you are using fresh sage, chop it coarsely first. Set the tenderloin aside for stuffing later.

6. Remove the prosciutto from the freezer and slice thinly for Chef Due. See how Chef Due is doing with the stuffing; can you lend a hand?

7. Invite Chef Due to help in stuffing the loin (it's a little like surgery). Using your fingers or a spoon, insert the stuffing into the pork pocket until fully stuffed. Secure the pork loin with twine or toothpicks (If you use toothpicks, run them under the water faucet for a minute, this will prevent them from burning in the oven). Set on a rack in a roasting pan. Pour a

1. Clean the mushrooms with a damp cloth or paper towel, and cut off the bottom of the stem. Coarsely chop the mushrooms.

2. Chop one onion (half for the stuffing, half for the potatoes, which you'll work on later), and mince the garlic clove.

3. Put a tablespoon of olive oil in a medium-sized frying pan over medium heat.

4. When the oil is hot, sauté half of the chopped onion and garlic until the onion is soft. Add the mushrooms, and if you happen to have the suggested glass of pinot grigio nearby, throw in a splash. Sauté until the mushrooms are soft.

5. Add several twists of freshly ground pepper to taste. Continue sautéing the stuffing for one more minute.

6. Add the sliced prosciutto (Chef Uno did this) to your stuffing and sauté an additional minute.

7. If Chef Uno doesn't need your help with the pork, start on the salad. Place

splash of wine over the pork, and put in the oven. Splash with wine every 10 minutes. You will want to check for doneness after 30 minutes. Wash your hands before you continue!

8. Check the potatoes in the microwave for doneness. They should be soft when you squeeze gently. Microwave for a few more minutes if necessary.

9. When the potatoes are done and cooled enough to handle with a paper towel, slice them in half lengthwise (carefully, to keep them whole for stuffing!), and scoop out the potato meat in a bowl. Make sure you save at least two perfect potato skins.

10. Add the butter to the potato meat while it's still hot; also add the cheese as soon as Chef Due is done grating. Stir well to melt the butter and cheese. Add the garlic, salt, chopped onion (Chef Due did this for you earlier), and pepper; stir.

11. Spoon the potato mixture back into the potato halves. Place on a baking sheet and put in the oven for the last 10 minutes of the pork cooking time.

12. Relax or set the table until the pork is ready.

13. The pork is done when the juices run clear when it's poked with a fork.

the sun-dried tomatoes in a bowl and cover with very hot water. If your sun-dried tomatoes are already packed in oil, make sure they are at room temperature.

8. Wash the greens and shake or spin dry. Arrange on salad plates.

9. Grate the cheese for the potatoes and set aside for Chef Uno.

10. When the tomatoes are soft, slice into strips. Add to the salad plates.

11. Using a knife or spoon, gently "chop" the goat cheese into small pieces.

12. Sprinkle the walnuts and goat cheese on the salad. Drizzle a little red wine vinegar on top. Top with freshly ground pepper. (You can substitute the vinegar with your favorite dressing, or use the recipe for vinaigrette found in A Celebration for Two Dinner Date.)

11. Trim the tough ends off the asparagus and place in a steamer or, if no steamer is available, place in a large frying pan and cover asparagus with water. Put on the stove top but don't steam yet! (You might want to ask Chef Uno if the pork should be basted.)

I like to also make a small slice into the meat and check for color. You want it not too pink and not too dark. Trust your instincts. Depending on the size of the pork loin and how fully stuffed it is, it should take between 30 and 40 minutes to cook. When it is done, remove from the rack, place on a cutting board, and cover loosely with foil. Make sure you save the juices in the roasting pan. Don't forget to remove the potatoes too!

14. Take the pork roasting pan and put on stove top. Turn the heat on high. Let Chef Due know that you are about to make the sherry sauce. Add sherry and butter to the pan, and stir in with pork pan juices over high heat until boiling. Reduce heat to medium and stir constantly until liquid is reduced by half.

15. For the presentation: slice the pork into ½-inch slices and fan out on a warm plate. Spoon sauce over the pork. Add asparagus, lemon wedge, and a potato to each plate. Have the salad either on the side or after your main course. Happy birthday!

12. Join Chef Uno in his or her step 12.

13. When Chef Uno begins to make the sherry sauce, turn the heat on under the asparagus. Check for doneness in 3 to 4 minutes. They should be soft but still crunchy.

14. Slice the lemon into wedges if you haven't already.

15. Open the wine, and happy birthday! Don't forget the dessert later.

Garlic Fest

World's Best Artichokes

Garlicky-Lemon Chicken

Avocado Halves with Cherry Tomatoes and Vinaigrette

Flageolets Pureed with Roasted Garlic

Assorted Sorbets

PREPARATION TIME

About 1^1/2 hours

You might think you'd have to be pretty brave to serve up a menu full of garlic for a dinner date. But hey, you're both doing it; you'll get good and garlicky together, so who cares? Besides, garlic is a perfect food: It tastes great, it's very good for you, and it smells incredible while you're cooking. So be brave and indulge yourself!

Dinner Date Hints

❥ Flageolets are French kidney-shaped beans that are white or pale green. They can be rather expensive and hard to find. However, I suggest you give it a try because they are well worth the effort and provide a wonderful taste sensation when blended with the roasted garlic. If you simply cannot find them, substitute any small white bean—navy or canelli, for example.

❥ When shopping for artichokes, chose heavy, green heads with leaves still tightly adhered to the bodies. They should not look or feel wilty. If this is your first time with artichokes, please read How to Eat an Artichoke in Helpful Hints.

❥ The avocado should be soft but not mushy when you gently squeeze it. Depending on the season, you may need to purchase the avocado a few days ahead in order to let it ripen. I always have a few avocados ripening in my fruit bowl.

❥ Try a Sancerre for your white wine. Ask for suggestions at your wine store.

❥ I suggest raspberry, lemon, or even mango (if you can find it) for the sorbets. You may want to serve the sorbet with a light cookie.

Shopping List

Staples

Olive oil

Butter

Balsamic vinegar

Dijon mustard

2–3 heads fresh garlic

Produce

2 large artichokes

1 lemon

1 avocado

6–8 cherry tomatoes

1 carrot

1 yellow onion

2–3 sprigs fresh thyme

1 bunch parsley

1 bunch fresh basil (optional)

2–3 sprigs fresh rosemary

Other

White wine (for drinking; see Dinner
  Date Hints)

Dry white wine (for cooking)

Dried dill

1 can chicken broth

1 cup flageolet beans

2–3 bay leaves

1 baguette

Assorted sorbets

Meat

2 chicken breasts, with skin and
  bone intact

Equipment List

2 medium-sized roasting pans

Food processor or blender

Host Prep

At the very least, plan to start the beans about two hours before your date arrives (see directions below). The flageolet beans do take the longest to cook, but they don't require any tending, so it is a relatively stress-free operation. You can prepare the beans up to the point of puree in advance, or you can have them simmering gently when your date arrives.

If you don't have a microwave, be sure to roast the whole head of garlic in a 375°F oven for approximately 45 minutes. (I actually prefer it this way.) Please see more about roasting garlic in Helpful Hints. You can probably time the garlic to be almost done by the time your date arrives. That way it can cool at room temperature and send its enticing aroma to greet your date. On the following page I've detailed steps for the beans up to the point of puree with garlic:

Flageolet Beans

1 cup flageolet beans

1 carrot, scrubbed and halved

1 yellow onion, peeled and halved

1 bouquet garni:

4–5 thyme and parsley sprigs with 2–3 bay leaves tied together in a bundle. Use butcher's twine to tie the bouquet together. In a pinch, I have been known to use unflavored dental floss to tie a bouquet garni together.

Salt to taste (½ teaspoon or more)

1. The night before your date, put the beans in a large pot and cover with cold water. Soak them overnight. If you are having a more spontaneous Dinner Date and don't have 12 to 24 extra hours to soak the beans, try this quick-soak method: Rinse beans, place in a large pot, and cover with cold water. Cover with lid and bring to a boil. Once boiling, remove the pot from heat and, keeping it covered, let it rest for 45 minutes. Continue with recipe as follows.

2. An hour or so before your date arrives, drain the beans from their soaking water, being sure to pick out any skins that may have floated to the top. Put beans back in the pot and cover again with fresh cold water, add the carrot, onion, and bouquet garni. Place over high heat and bring to a boil, then reduce heat, simmer, and forget about it for 1 hour.

3. After 1 hour, begin testing for tenderness. Add salt to taste, and continue to simmer until tender (about 30 minutes).

4. When the beans are done, drain and save a cup of the cooking liquid. Discard the vegetables and bouquet garni. Set aside until ready to puree.

The Dinner Date

Marinating the Chefs

You are going to need to open a bottle of white wine with which to baste the chicken, so you might as well open a bottle and have a glass while you are cooking. Make sure it is dry but not too overpowering. Try a Sauvignon Blanc.

World's Best Artichokes

2 large artichokes

4–6 uncooked garlic cloves

Olive oil

Salt

Freshly ground pepper

Garlicky-Lemon Chicken

2 chicken breasts

2 garlic cloves, sliced

4–8 garlic cloves, whole

Fresh rosemary sprigs

1 lemon

Olive oil

White wine

Salt

Freshly ground pepper

Avocado Halves

1 avocado
6–8 cherry tomatoes
Fresh basil

Vinaigrette

Olive oil
Balsamic vinegar
Dijon mustard
Freshly ground pepper
Salt
Dried dill

Flageolets Pureed with Roasted Garlic

Prepared flageolet beans
(see Host Prep)
Olive oil
3/4 cup bean cooking liquid
1/4 cup chicken broth
1 head garlic
2 tablespoons butter
Salt
Freshly ground pepper

1. Preheat oven to 400°F for the chicken.

2. Peel and thinly slice the garlic cloves for both the artichokes and chicken.

3. Work with Chef Due to place a slice of garlic in between each leaf of artichoke. It takes a while to accomplish this, but you'll be happy you were so thorough. Work from the outside inward, until you can't pry the center leaves open.

4. Wash and pat dry the chicken breasts.

5. With your fingers, make room between the meat and skin of the chicken and slide garlic slices inside. Do the same with the rosemary. After you're done be sure to wash your hands!

6. Combine the juice from ½ lemon and 1 tablespoon of olive oil in a bowl. Stir well with a fork.

7. Using your fingers (again!) spread the olive oil mixture on the chicken, making sure to cover the entire breast.

1. Rinse the artichokes thoroughly. Slice the top ½ inch off the head of artichoke and spread the leaves out as best as you can. Slice the bottom stem close to the head, so that the artichoke is flat on the bottom and can stand by itself.

2. See Chef Uno step 3. It is important that you both do this step, because then each of you will have garlicky hands and won't have to feel embarrassed about it.

3. Place the artichokes in a shallow roasting pan and drizzle olive oil over each; don't be shy about it!

4. Salt and pepper each artichoke heavily.

5. Put enough water in the pan to cover about 1 inch of the artichokes and place on a burner.

6. Loosely tent the pan with aluminum foil so that the artichokes are basically steamed, but a little steam can escape. Place over high heat, and when it boils, turn heat to medium.

7. Steam for about 40 minutes. Artichokes are done when the leaves pull easily away from the head. Keep an eye on the water in the pan as they cook, and add more if it's running low.

8. Place the chicken in a roasting pan and cover with enough white wine to fill the pan up to about $1/2$ inch, squeeze the remaining lemon on top, and tuck the whole garlic cloves as best you can in and around the chicken. Use as many whole cloves as you think you can stand. Salt and pepper the chicken.

9. Place in preheated oven. Check in 10 minutes, and pour more wine over the top. The chicken will take about 20 to 25 minutes to cook. To see if it is done, poke it in the thickest places, and make sure the juices run clear.

10. If you have chosen to oven roast the garlic, ignore this step. But if you are going to microwave the garlic, start by chopping the very top off the garlic head, and place it on a microwavable plate. Pierce some of the cloves with a knife and wrap the whole head loosely in a paper towel. Microwave on high 40 seconds, then turn the garlic over and microwave another 30 seconds.

11. As soon as the garlic is cool enough to handle, squeeze the softened garlic cloves out of their skins and into a skillet.

12. Put the beans, a bit of olive oil and $1/4$ cup of the bean cooking liquid

8. See if Chef Uno needs any help with the chicken. Better yet, see if Chef Uno needs to be remarinated.

9. Cut the avocado in half lengthwise and remove the pit. Place each half on a salad plate.

10. Wash and remove stems from the cherry tomatoes. Cut them in quarters, and place in and around the avocado. Garnish with fresh basil if desired.

11. On to the vinaigrette: The secret to making a good vinaigrette is in the proportions. Just keep adding ingredients until you get it to taste right. The basic rule is two parts oil to one part vinegar. Start by combining $1/2$ cup olive oil, $1/4$ cup vinegar, and a tablespoon Dijon mustard in a bowl. Add some grindings of pepper, a dash of salt, and a sprinkling of dill. Stir well with a fork until the oil no longer separates from the other ingredients. Taste, and go from there!

12. Check the water in the artichoke pan! Add more if it's getting low.

13. Sauté the garlic for the beans that Chef Uno has put in the skillet in a tablespoon of olive oil. As you sauté, use a wooden spoon to break up the soft garlic cloves.

(which you set aside earlier) into a food processor or blender and puree. Add ¼ cup chicken broth and puree. You want to get a nice but still coarse consistency, with a thickness about like mashed potatoes. Add more bean cooking liquid if the mixture is too thick.

13. Add the bean mixture to the garlic sauté that Chef Due has prepared.

14. When the chicken is done, check on the artichokes. Keep the chicken warm by covering the pan with foil until artichokes are ready. If you have prepared some rather large artichokes, you may want to start with the chicken and beans and have the artichokes 5 or 10 minutes into the meal when they are done.

15. When serving the chicken, spoon the cooking juices over the chicken.

16. See tips on eating artichokes in the appendix, get messy and ENJOY!

17. When you are ready for dessert, serve the sorbet.

18. In the days to come, be careful not to breathe too heavily on people you don't know well!

14. Once the beans have been added to the garlic, add the two tablespoons of butter and stir well to thoroughly combine with the garlic and beans. Let the butter melt and the beans heat through. Season with salt and pepper to taste. (Ask Chef Uno to taste too!) If, after the beans are ready, you find yourselves waiting for the chicken or the artichokes, turn off the heat and cover the beans. You can reheat the beans when you are ready.

15. Just before you sit down to eat, drizzle some vinaigrette on the avocado halves. Or if you want to save the avocados for a second course (it can be refreshing after all that garlic!) drizzle right before eating.

16. Make sure there is a bowl on the table for the artichoke leaves!

17. Don't forget to put the bread on the table.

18. See Chef Uno steps 16, 17, and 18.

Indoor Picnic

Assorted Cheese and Pâté Platter

Baguette

Assortment of Olives and Cornichons

Fruit Slices

Chilled Asparagus

Sliced Prosciutto or Salami

Assorted Cookies

PREPARATION TIME

About 15 minutes (not including shopping!)

Lance and I celebrated our first wedding anniversary on a rainy July day in our little (and I mean *little*) New York City apartment. We were not daunted by the weather or our specific confines, and we used a lovely picnic basket (a wedding gift) to help set the stage for a living room feast. We spread a blanket on the floor, moved a bouquet of flowers down to our level, and opened a bottle of indulgent Dom Perignon (also a wedding gift!). Indoor picnicking has since turned into a tradition for us, and I hope you will have as much fun with it as we have had!

This Dinner Date is somewhat different in that very little cooking is required. So, why not begin your date with a trip to a gourmet deli or grocer where you can shop together for your Dinner Date picnic? Enjoy the exotic sights and smells of the cheese selection. Some delis will let you sample, so make an adventure of it. Since so little prep work is required here, before your shopping trip find your picnic paradise and prepare to set a sumptuous table—I mean floor. Though this menu is entitled *Indoor* Picnic, you could certainly take it outdoors if the weather allows.

Dinner Date Hints and More

✦ Please do your shopping at a gourmet deli or grocer and ask for advice on cheese and pâté. Try to get 2 or 3 different cheeses and 1 or 2 different patés. You'll want at least one soft cheese, Brie or Camembert, for example, and one harder one. Use your personal taste; I love ripe, pungent cheeses like a Roquefort or Morbier (called stinky cheese by my husband—and he has got a point there).

✦ Pâté comes in two textures, usually called country pâté and mousse pâté. Country pâté will have a courser look to it and is wonderful hunked on some fresh bread with a smear of Dijon mustard on top. Mousse pâté is smooth and rich and incredibly indulgent. A duck or goose liver pâté would be most elegant.

- Buy fresh French bread. You may also want to supplement the bread with an assortment of crackers. If you do, try to get simply flavored ones that won't overpower the taste of the delicious cheeses and meats that you buy.

- Most deli shops now offer Greek-, Italian-, and French-style olives. Get a nice selection. Also, cornichons (which are small gherkinlike pickles) are a nice, crisp complement to the rich cheese and pâté.

- Buy crisp apples and ripe strawberries if they are in season.

- Asparagus may be hard to find (at a reasonable price) when not in season. If so, substitute with a selection of crudité (broccoli florets, carrot and celery sticks).

- Again, seek out advice on the prosciutto and salami. Get a nice selection. Prosciutto is very flavorful, so you won't need much. If you and your date aren't big meat eaters, see if your gourmet deli offers any exciting salads or grilled vegetables to go.

- Use your personal taste for the cookie assortment. You and your date will probably be very full by the time you get to dessert, so remember that your eyes may be bigger than your stomach at the store!

- I love champagne with a picnic. Buy it beforehand and make sure it is well chilled. You could also try a chardonnay or Sauvignon Blanc. Anything goes here, so pick your favorite.

- If you will be dining al fresco (outside), make the asparagus ahead of time and keep it chilled in the fridge.

- A nice touch is to wrap the asparagus in slices of prosciutto. It is a wonderful combo.

Aside from all the items mentioned above, it is a must to have the following on hand for a great picnic:

Assorted mustards (course grain, Dijon, honey or fruit-flavored)
Butter
Balsamic vinegar (to drizzle on the asparagus)

Marinating the Chefs

You could always pop the champagne and have a glass while you arrange your picnic platters.

Steamed Asparagus

1 pound asparagus

1. Snap the tougher ends off the asparagus. Place in steamer basket over pan of water (if basket is available), or cover with cold water in a pan. Place over high heat. Asparagus is done when it is just tender when pricked with a fork. Careful not to overcook!

2. Slice the bread and arrange attractively on a plate.

3. Arrange the meats on a plate.

4. See Chef Due step 4!

1. Unwrap the cheese and arrange on a platter with pâté.

2. Slice the fruit and arrange attractively on cheese platter.

3. Place the just-cooked asparagus in cool water, then transfer to a plate. Drizzle balsamic vinegar on top if desired.

4. Bring all plates and platters to the pre-set picnic area and enjoy!

The Ultimate Valentine's Day Dinner

French Onion Soup

Filet Mignon with Herbed Butter

Sautéed Mushrooms

Simply Steamed Spinach

Garlic Mashed Potatoes

Chocolate-Dipped Strawberries and Biscotti

PREPARATION TIME

About 1 hour

Invite your Valentine over to the most exclusive, romantic place in town. No need to wait for February 14, however; this Dinner Date can be put to good use whenever you want to create the romance of Valentine's Day.

Dinner Date Hints

- ❧ If you, like me, live in a part of the world where February 14 is usually a cold day, you may think I am crazy for suggesting this, but if at all possible, try to grill the steaks outside. Steaks taste so great on the barbecue, and the aroma will remind you both that spring is not *that* far away. If grilling is an impossibility, an oven broiler is fine.

- ❧ If you can, buy large, plump strawberries. If the strawberry selection is disappointing, find a nice selection of imported (Belgian or French) chocolates to serve instead.

- ❧ Follow your taste buds when it comes to the dipping chocolate for the strawberries. Milk chocolate works well, but semisweet or even white chocolate can be delicious when combined with fresh strawberries.

- ❧ Biscotti are Italian cookies that are traditionally served with coffee. You can find them at most upscale grocers.

- ❧ You are going to need oven-proof bowls for the onion soup (see equipment list). Many home furnishing stores sell crocks specifically for onion soup.

- ❧ For a special Valentine's Day touch, you could try cutting heart-shaped toasts for the onion soup. A heart-shaped cookie cutter will do this, or a skilled artist's hand.

- ❧ Try a merlot or pinot noir for your red wine choice.

Staples

Olive oil

Fresh garlic

Salt

Freshly ground pepper

Garlic powder

All-purpose flour

Dried rosemary

Produce

2 large white onions

Fresh parsley

2 Idaho baking potatoes

1 bag triple-washed spinach

10 white mushrooms

12 large strawberries

Dairy and Meat

Butter

Unsalted butter

Gruyère cheese

2 filets mignons

Milk

Other

2 cans beef broth

8 ounces chocolate

Biscotti

1 baguette

Red wine

Champagne and Chambord
(optional, see Marinating the
Chefs)

Equipment List

2 soup crocks

Broiler pan (if using the broiler, but I
hope you have a grill you can use)

Steamer basket

Wax paper

Potato masher

Heart-shaped cookie cutter

Double boiler (a bowl that fits—or
rests comfortably on top of—a pot
with water in it)

Host Prep

There is very little to do ahead of time except
for setting a very romantic table. If you don't
have a microwave, you can oven roast the garlic. Check out Helpful Hints for instructions.

The Dinner Date

Marinating the Chefs

Try a Kir Royale, which is a pretty and appropriately pink cocktail for Valentine's Day. Fill a glass with champagne, and add a splash of Chambord (raspberry liqueur). You can tone it down, if you like, to a regular Kir by using white wine instead of champagne. A nonalcoholic version can be made with seltzer water and Italian raspberry-flavored syrup.

Onion Soup

2 large white onions

6 tablespoons unsalted butter

1 tablespoon all-purpose flour

2 cans (about 4 cups) beef broth

Salt

Freshly ground pepper

2–4 slices baguette

1 cup shredded Gruyère cheese

Chocolate-Dipped Strawberries

12 beautiful strawberries

8 ounces chocolate

Filet Mignon with Herbed Butter

2 filets mignons

Salt (optional)

Freshly ground pepper (optional)

About 1 teaspoon garlic powder

1 stick butter

$\frac{1}{4}$ cup chopped parsley

About $\frac{1}{2}$ teaspoon dried rosemary

Garlic Mashed Potatoes

2 Idaho baking potatoes

2–3 tablespoons butter

1 head garlic

$\frac{1}{2}$–1 cup milk at room temperature

Sautéed Mushrooms

$\frac{1}{2}$ pound white mushrooms

Olive oil

1–2 cloves garlic

Salt

Freshly ground pepper

Simply Steamed Spinach

1 bag triple-washed spinach

1. Cut the onions in half at the stem. Lay the halves down flat and cut thin slices.

2. In a large soup pot, melt the butter over low heat, then add the onions, turn up the heat to medium and sauté. After a minute or so add the flour and continue to sauté until the onions have a nice golden color.

3. Add the beef broth and season with salt and pepper. (Unless you bought low-sodium broth, you won't need much salt.) Bring to a boil.

4. Once the soup has boiled, turn the heat down and let the onions cook for about 15 minutes. Stir occasionally. Turn heat off when onions are cooked and leave on burner for reheating later.

5. Wash the strawberries well, leaving the stems on, and dry with a paper towel.

6. Help Chef Due with the strawberry dipping.

7. Wash and chop the parsley. Set aside for Chef Due.

8. Season the steaks in any way you

1. Set a stick of salted butter out to soften, for the herbed butter.

2. Grate the cheese for the onion soup and set aside.

3. If you are going all out and doing the heart-shaped baguette slices (see Dinner Date Hints), do this now. It's okay if you get some crust in your heart shape because it adds a nice texture in the soup. Set these aside.

4. Melt the chocolate over medium heat in a double boiler (a bowl that just fits in a pan with 2 inches of water in it). Move on to step 5, but stir the chocolate a few times until it's all melted.

5. Prepare a cookie sheet or plate lined with wax paper for the strawberries. Make sure there is room in the fridge for the cookie sheet!

6. Once the chocolate has melted, dip the strawberries in until they are $2/3$ covered. You may need to roll the strawberry a bit depending on the depth of the bowl. Remove and let the strawberries drip a bit in the bowl and then lay carefully on the wax paper.

7. Once all strawberries are dipped, place cookie sheet in fridge.

8. Remember that stick of butter you got out of the fridge? Well, put it in a

prefer. Some people are real purists and don't season at all. I would suggest sprinkling some salt on the meat and giving a few twists of the pepper mill. You can also add garlic powder, or even insert fresh garlic slices into the meat after carefully making small incisions all over it. Once seasoned, set the steaks aside.

9. Peel and cut the potatoes into about 1-inch pieces. Set these aside. You will finish the mashed potatoes later so they will be piping hot and ready to eat.

10. Wash the mushrooms carefully, cutting off the stems. Slice and set aside.

11. Even though the spinach is triple washed, rinse it again, and pull off leaf stems. Place in steamer basket and put in pot with 2 inches water. Set this aside.

12. Preheat the broiler. If you are grilling your steaks, get the grill going.

13. Set a pot ⅔ filled with water over high heat, and bring to a boil for the potatoes.

14. When water boils, add the potatoes and cook until tender (10 to 15 minutes). The potatoes will cook while you eat your soup.

small bowl and cream it with a wooden spoon. Add the chopped parsley (Chef Uno did this for you), rosemary and garlic powder to taste. For a real treat, hold off on the garlic until you're roasting fresh garlic for the mashed potatoes, then add a fresh roasted clove and stir well into the butter. Once all ingredients have been added to your liking, scrape the butter into a small dish and refrigerate. I use ramekins, which are small souffle or custard dishes.

9. If the garlic was not oven-roasted, prepare the garlic for the microwave by chopping the top (that's the narrow part) off the head and then pricking all around with a knife. Wrap loosely in a paper towel and put on a microwave-safe plate. Microwave 40 seconds on one side, then turn over and microwave an additional 30 seconds. Squeeze the garlic gently; if it still feels a little hard, microwave an additional 15 seconds. When cool enough to handle, separate the cloves from the skin. Set aside.

10. Reheat the onion soup over medium-low heat.

11. Finely chop 1 to 2 garlic cloves for the mushrooms.

15. With the broiler still going, put in the steaks (or throw them on the grill) now. Please also note Chef Due step 15.

16. Hope you enjoyed the soup! While the steaks are finishing up, drain the potatoes and place in a large bowl. Add 2 to 3 tablespoons of butter, 5 to 6 roasted garlic cloves and ¼ cup milk. Mash with potato masher until all ingredients are blended. Taste and add more milk for smoothness, more garlic and salt and pepper if desired. Place in covered dish and bring to the table.

17. Serve the steaks with a blanket of mushrooms and chunk of herbed butter on top.

18. Open the wine and enjoy!

12. In a sauté pan, heat 1 tablespoon or so of olive oil. Add chopped garlic and sauté till just golden. Add the mushrooms and sauté until soft. Season with salt and pepper. Remove from heat. You can reheat later if necessary.

13. How is Chef Uno doing? You are both at the final stages here, so make sure you are in sync. Once the broiler is heated, ladle the onion soup into the soup crocks. Add one or two baguette slices and top with grated cheese. Broil for 2 minutes or until the cheese bubbles and browns slightly.

14. Remove the crocks and bring to table—careful, the crocks will be *very* hot!

15. One of you will have to check the steaks and turn them over during your soup course. The time for this will vary depending on how you like your steaks cooked and how thick they are: 5 to 7 minutes on each side for rare, 7 to 9 for medium, 9 to 11 for well. If you are cooking a well-done steak (which I personally hope you aren't, but it's your choice!), Chef Uno's potatoes will probably be ready before the steaks and he or she should proceed with step 16.

16. Just before steaks are done, place the spinach over high heat and steam until just dark green and tender.

17. Reheat the mushrooms.

18. Slice the rest of the baguette and place on table. Enjoy!

Catch of the Day

Almost Caesar Salad

Salmon Steaks with Dijon Sauce

Elegant Potatoes

Snow Peas

Individual Apple Crisps

PREPARATION TIME

About 1 hour

It doesn't get any simpler or more elegant than this! Surprise your date with this menu after a peaceful Saturday spent biking, skating, or walking in the park.

Dinner Date Hints

- Make sure the salmon steaks you get are about 1-inch thick.

- Buy the smallest potatoes you can find, preferably Red Bliss.

- Try Golden Delicious or Granny Smith apples, or whatever is your favorite. I like to use a variety of apples.

- The salad is "almost" Caesar because of the missing anchovies. If you are a big anchovy fan, please feel free to add them when you are adding the Parmesan cheese. I find that most of my friends ask me to omit them, so it is with that in mind that I omitted them here.

- If you can, grill the salmon on a charcoal or gas grill. If this is not possible, use your broiler.

- Mustard seeds can be found in the spice section of your grocery store.

- Serve a rich, full-bodied chardonnay with this menu.

- Serve with hot rolls from the bakery or grocery store.

Shopping List

Staples

Olive oil
Fresh garlic
Brown sugar
Dijon mustard
Salt
Freshly ground pepper
Cinnamon
Flour
Garlic powder

Produce

Romaine lettuce
8–10 small potatoes
1/2 pound snow peas
1 lemon
3 apples
1 shallot
1 bunch parsley
2–3 sprigs fresh rosemary

Dairy and Meat

2 salmon steaks
Heavy cream

1 egg
Butter
Fresh Parmesan cheese
Ice cream (optional)
Whipped cream (optional)

Other

Croutons
Tabasco sauce
Mustard seed
Chardonnay
Rolls
Cooking sherry
Slivered almonds

Equipment List

Salad bowl
Gas or charcoal grill (if available)
Steamer basket
2 small baking dishes (for the individual apple crisps)

Host Prep

No preparation necessary!

The Dinner Date

Marinating the Chefs

Open that bottle of chardonnay early and toast each other before you begin to cook.

Salmon Steaks

2 salmon steaks

Olive oil

Garlic powder

Salt

Freshly ground pepper

1 sprig fresh rosemary

Elegant Potatoes

8–10 small potatoes

1 handful parsley

3–5 tablespoons butter

Snow Peas

½ pound snow peas

1 tablespoon butter

2 tablespoons slivered almonds

Almost Caesar Salad

1 egg

1 garlic clove

Pinch and a half salt

1 teaspoon mustard

1 tablespoon lemon juice

Tabasco sauce

1 tablespoon olive oil

1 bunch romaine lettuce

1–2 tablespoons Parmesan cheese

Croutons

Dijon Sauce

1 shallot

1 tablespoon olive oil

1 cup heavy cream

$\frac{1}{4}$ cup cooking sherry

3–4 tablespoons Dijon mustard

1 tablespoon mustard seed

Individual Apple Crisps

3 apples

$\frac{1}{4}$ cup flour

$\frac{1}{4}$ cup brown sugar

3 tablespoons butter

$\frac{1}{2}$ teaspoon cinnamon

1. If you will be grilling the salmon steaks, start the grill now.

2. Rub a small amount of olive oil on each salmon steak. Dust with garlic powder, and sprinkle salt and pepper on both sides. Wash and remove the rosemary leaves from each sprig and gently rub these into each steak. Cover and refrigerate.

3. Wash and snap the snow peas. Make sure you remove all the stringy parts from the sides! You should be able to do this in one movement; snap one end and pull down, removing the string, kind of like opening a Band-Aid.

4. Place these in a steamer basket inside a pot. Fill the pot with water to just below the steamer basket. Set aside.

5. Wash the romaine lettuce and let Chef Due know when it is well rinsed.

6. On to the Dijon sauce. Chop the shallot well.

7. Put the olive oil for the sauce in a sauté pan and heat over medium heat. Add shallots when hot, then sauté.

1. Scrub the potatoes and cut them in half crosswise. Place them in a pot. Cover the potatoes with water and put on high heat. Cover the pot. Check in about 7 minutes.

2. Clean the parsley and cut off the stems. Coarsely chop the parsley leaves. Set aside.

3. Put a small pot of water on to boil for the egg in your salad. Once the water is boiling, add the egg and continue to boil for about 1 minute.

4. Get out the salad bowl you will be using. Peel and crush slightly the garlic clove. You can do this by placing the flat side of your knife on the clove and hitting it with the palm of your hand once, hard.

5. Sprinkle the salt in the bottom of the bowl and rub it in with your garlic clove. Discard the garlic.

6. Add the mustard, lemon juice, a dash of Tabasco, and the olive oil, then mix well.

7. Once the romaine lettuce is cleaned, add this to the salad bowl and

8. Once the shallots are soft, add the cream and stir. Let the cream come to a boil and then turn the heat to low. Let the cream simmer until it is reduced by at least ⅓ (about 3 to 4 minutes).

9. Meanwhile, put the mustard seeds in a small frying pan and toast them over medium heat. Once they begin to pop and crackle, remove immediately from the heat and pour into a small bowl. Put this aside.

10. If you are going to be broiling the salmon, preheat the broiler now.

11. Once the cream is reduced, stir in the mustard and sherry. Continue stirring over low heat for a few minutes. Add the mustard seed. Turn the heat off and cover. You will reheat the sauce soon. Add more mustard to taste.

12. Get ready to cook the salmon. If you are grilling, slightly oil the cooking grate. Whether grilling or broiling, cook about 5 to 6 minutes on each side.

13. When you turn the steaks, put the snow peas on the stove over high heat. Turn the heat on low under the mustard sauce.

14. Once the salmon steaks are done (you want them to be tender and flake with a fork), remove from the grill or broiler and wrap in foil to keep warm while you finish the snow peas.

toss well. Set this aside for finishing touches at the table.

8. Check the potatoes by piercing one with a fork. If there is no resistance, remove the pot from the heat and drain the water out of the pot. Return the potatoes to the pot and toss with the butter and parsley. Cover and set aside.

9. Get the rolls ready to be heated. If you are broiling the salmon, wrap the rolls in foil and put in the oven while it heats. If you are grilling, heat the rolls in a 325°F oven for 10 to 12 minutes.

10. Peel, quarter, and core the apples.

11. Slice each apple quarter into 4 slices.

12. Divide the apple slices into the two individual oven-proof dishes. Dot with 1 tablespoon of the butter.

13. In a small bowl, combine the flour, brown sugar, remaining butter (2 tablespoons), and cinnamon. Work the ingredients together with your fingers or a fork.

14. Sprinkle the topping over the apples, dividing equally between the two dishes.

15. When the snow peas turn a pretty dark green color and are tender (they should still crunch slightly), put them in a serving bowl and toss with butter and the almonds until the butter is melted. This dish is ready for the table.

16. Place each salmon steak along with the potatoes on a plate. Pour a little of the mustard sauce over the salmon, and put the remaining sauce in a sauce boat (or bowl) for extras at the table.

17. Don't forget the rolls!

18. Sit down, eat, and enjoy!

15. The apple crisps cook in a 375°F oven. If you are grilling, put them in the oven now. If not, wait until the salmon is done and then reduce the heat to 375°. They should cook for about 20 minutes, or until golden brown.

16. Time to finish the Caesar salad. Bring the bowl and remaining ingredients (egg, Parmesan cheese, and croutons) to the table.

17. Sprinkle the cheese, then crack the egg over the salad. Toss well to mix. Add the croutons, and you are ready!

18. Sit down, eat, and enjoy! Don't forget the apple crisps. Remove them from the oven when they are done and set aside until ready. Don't worry if you don't eat them for a while, they are just as good at room temperature. You can serve with ice cream or whipped cream if desired.

Gotta Grill

Greek Salad

Build-Your-Own Kebabs

Rice Pilaf

Ambrosia

PREPARATION TIME
About 1 hour

This menu is perfect for pleasing any food preference and can adapt to any foreseeable diet. You're a vegetarian and she's not? You're a rare meat lover and he's not? Don't let different approaches to food get between you and your *amore;* make this menu and everyone goes home happy, or maybe not (. . . goes home, that is).

Dinner Date Hints

- Of the multitudes of kebab-able items offered here, pick a selection of 4 to 5 veggies and 2 to 3 meats. You don't want to overwhelm your guest with choices, or have so many leftovers you'll be kebab-ing it for days.

- If you don't have access to an outdoor grill, use the broiler in your oven.

- Try to buy fresh feta cheese from a deli rather than packaged feta from a grocery store.

- If you are cooking for a vegetarian, substitute a vegetable broth for chicken in the rice.

- Try a Greek rosé wine (like Roditis) to go with your meal.

- If you and your date are in the mood for an indulgent dessert, pick up some baklava at your nearest Greek deli.

- A small amount of store-bought humus with some pita wedges provides a good munchie for while you are cooking.

- If you can find some Greek music, play it!

Shopping List

(See next page for marinade shopping lists)

Staples

Olive oil
Salt
Onion salt
Freshly ground pepper
Dijon mustard
Long-grain rice

Produce

4 plum tomatoes
1 cucumber
1 yellow onion
3 oranges
1 lemon
Any of the following:
  White mushrooms
  Portobello mushrooms
  Zucchini
  Yellow squash
  Red or yellow cherry tomatoes
  Yellow or red onions
  Eggplant
  Red, yellow, or green peppers

Dairy and Meat

Feta cheese
Butter
Any of the following:
  Large shrimp
  Tuna steak
  Lamb chop (2 small, boned)
  Steak
  Chicken breast

Other

1 can chicken broth
Orzo or angel hair pasta
Kalamata olives
Orange liqueur
Shredded coconut (unsweetened)
Humus (optional)
Pita bread (optional)
Imported beer (optional, see Marinating the Chefs)

Equipment List

Skewers
Charcoal or gas grill

Marinade shopping lists

For the chicken:
    Sun-dried tomatoes
    Fresh basil
    Fresh garlic

For the steak, lamb, and shrimp:
    Garlic powder
    Onion salt
    Paprika

For the tuna steak:
    Sesame oil
    Soy sauce
    Fresh ginger
    Fresh garlic

Host Prep

If you have opted for either the chicken or the tuna steak, it is best to marinate these a minimum of 2 hours before your date arrives.

The marinades for the steak, lamb, or shrimp can be prepared during your Dinner Date.

Chicken Marinade

1–2 chicken breasts (opt for more if this is your only meat)

1–2 tablespoons olive oil

1–2 tablespoons Dijon mustard

1 tablespoon lemon juice

5–6 sun-dried tomatoes

1 bunch fresh basil

2 cloves garlic

1. Cut the chicken into 1-2-inch cubes. Set aside.

2. In a bowl, combine olive oil, mustard, and lemon juice. Mix well.

3. Reconstitute the sun-dried tomatoes if necessary (place in a bowl and cover in boiling water for 5 minutes or until soft). Chop and add to oil and mustard mixture.

4. Coarsely chop the basil and add to marinade.

5. Mince the garlic and add to marinade. Mix well.

6. Add the chicken cubes and toss to make sure all the chicken is coated. Add more oil and mustard to the chicken if needed. Cover the bowl with plastic wrap and refrigerate for two hours.

Tuna Steak Marinade

1–2 tuna steaks (opt for more if tuna is your only meat)

1–2 tablespoons sesame oil

3–4 tablespoons soy sauce

1–2 teaspoons chopped ginger root

2 cloves garlic

1. Cut the tuna steak into 1-2-inch cubes. Set aside.

2. Combine sesame oil and soy sauce in a bowl.

3. Finely chop the ginger root (cut off a piece of the root, trim the brown exterior away, and mince). Add to marinade.

4. Mince the garlic and add to marinade.

5. Add the tuna cubes and toss. Add more soy if necessary. Cover and refrigerate for two hours.

Marinating the Chefs

Most people I know like to have a beer in hand when they grill. In keeping with the Aegean theme of the menu, you could buy some imported Greek beer or a sampling from various countries.

Build-Your-Own Kebabs

Selection of veggies and meats made from the shopping lists

Rice Pilaf

1 tablespoon olive oil

¼ cup orzo or angel hair pasta (break the angel hair into 2-inch-long pieces before measuring)

½ cup long-grain rice

1 cup chicken broth

1 tablespoon butter

Salt

Greek Salad

4 plum tomatoes

1 cucumber

1 yellow onion

2 tablespoons olive oil

1 tablespoon lemon juice

Salt

Freshly ground pepper

Feta cheese

6–8 Kalamata olives

Ambrosia

3 oranges

¼ cup shredded coconut

1–2 tablespoons orange liqueur

Chef Numero Uno

1. Start chopping the selected vegetables into skewer-able chunks. Keep the chopped vegetables separate for easy skewering later.

2. If you are preparing the steak or lamb, cut these into cubes.

3. If you are preparing the shrimp, shell, clean, and devein them.

4. In a medium-sized saucepan, heat the olive oil for the rice. Add the pasta and sauté until golden brown. Don't let it burn!

5. Add the rice and stir to coat. Add the stock and bring to a boil.

6. Once it boils, cover and turn heat down to simmer. Set timer for 15 minutes to check. You want to see all the liquid absorbed. Stir in the butter when done. Salt to taste.

7. Peel the oranges for the Ambrosia like you would an apple: with a knife in a spiral fashion. Make sure you get not only the peel but the white pith as well.

8. Slice the peeled oranges into rounds, and then slice the rounds in half. Place in a bowl and set aside.

Chef Numero Due

1. Help Chef Uno with the chopping.

2. If you are preparing either the steak, lamb, or shrimp, spread them out on a cookie sheet and sprinkle generous amounts of garlic powder, onion salt, paprika, and freshly ground pepper on the cubes (see marinades). Turn each piece and sprinkle spices on again.

3. If preparing the chicken or tuna, remove these from the fridge now.

4. Start the grill or broiler.

5. Chop the tomato, cucumber, and onion into small, bite-size pieces. Combine in a bowl.

6. In a small bowl, mix olive oil and lemon juice. Pour over the salad and season with salt and freshly ground pepper. Toss well.

7. Crumble the feta cheese on top and add the olives.

8. Join Chef Uno in the kebab assembly line. Alternate meat with vegetable, getting a nice variety of color. You may need to advise Chef Uno on these aesthetic issues.

9. Once the grill (or broiler) is good and hot, begin preparing your own personal kebab(s).

10. Once you and Chef Due have created your kebabs, stick them on the grill. Turn frequently. (if you feel you need a way to tell your kebabs apart, tear off a small piece of aluminum foil and attach to the skewer in a symbolic, perhaps artistic way.)

11. The kebabs will not take terribly long to cook, about 10 minutes, depending on the size of the cubed food and how well done you like your meat. Monitor the chicken; it may take a little longer and will be done when juices run clear after poking with a fork.

12. ENJOY!

9. Check the rice Chef Uno started. Is it done (is all the liquid absorbed)? If so, stir in 1 tablespoon of butter, and cover to keep it warm.

10. If there is time to kill waiting for the kebabs, you can start eating your Greek salad, or save it to eat during the rest of your meal.

11. When you are ready for dessert, sprinkle coconut and liqueur on the sliced oranges, toss lightly, and ENJOY!

Everyone Loves Pasta, the Sequel

Tomato and Onion Salad in an Avocado Shell with

Stealth Dressing

Fettucini with Mushroom Sauce

Parmesan Bread

Fresh Berries with Sabayon Sauce

PREPARATION TIME

About ½ hour

I call the salad dressing used in this menu "stealth dressing" because a certain amount of reconnaissance and espionage went into its invention. If I were to disclose how it came into being (involving a hotel, a small amount of purloined oil and vinegar, and a suspicious bartender), I fear there could be repercussions on a global scale. Let's just say that Lance and I were on an island off the coast of Spain and in desperate need of salad dressing to complement a picnic planned for our hotel room balcony. Much as any good husband and citizen would do in such circumstances, Lance went out into the world to find the needed items and returned triumphant 15 minutes later. I didn't ask the details (then), I only enjoyed the results of his secret mission.

Dinner Date Hints

- If you can find freshly made fettucini, please buy it. Or if you and your date are feeling extra adventurous, make your own (see Helpful Hints).

- You may be very fortunate and have an inventive produce section in the market where you shop. If so, use this menu to try every single mushroom variety they carry. If white button mushrooms are all that are available, they will do fine.

- Fresh Parmesan cheese, please!

- Make sure the avocado you prepare is barely soft when you gently squeeze it.

- Try a light, crisp pinot grigio as your wine selection.

- Buy a nice selection of berries, whatever looks good at the grocer. Make sure to have a little variation in color so your date will feel aesthetically fulfilled as well as just plain comfortably full.

- Sabayon sauce is a custardy sauce made with sherry, or marsala wine. You'll need to make it ahead of time, but you can refrigerate it for up to three days and serve it cold. If you want a shortcut, serve the berries with good old reliable whipped cream.

Staples

Olive oil

Fresh garlic

Dried oregano

Garlic powder (optional)

Red wine vinegar

Sugar

Salt

Freshly ground pepper

Produce

Mushroom selection

4–8 ounces each of any of the following for a total weight of about 1½ pounds:

white button

crimini

shiitaki

portobello

1 avocado

1 yellow onion

1 plum tomato

Fresh berries

1 bunch fresh basil

Dairy

4 eggs

Butter

Fresh Parmesan cheese

Whipping cream

Other

½ pound fettucini

1 can chicken or vegetable broth

Marsala or dry sherry

Pinot grigio

½ ounce dried porcini mushrooms

Italian bread

Italian beer (optional, see Marinating the Chefs)

Equipment List

Double boiler

Cheese grater

Host Prep

The Sabayon sauce requires a little elbow grease, as you'll be whisking the sauce constantly until it is ready, but it is worth it, I assure you. You can make this up to three days in advance, just make sure you keep it refrigerated. The recipe follows:

Sabayon Sauce

3 tablespoons whipping cream

4 egg yolks (for tips on separating eggs, see Helpful Tips)

¾ cup sugar

¾ cup marsala or dry sherry

1. Fill a large pan or baking dish with cracked ice and set aside. You will be cooling the sauce in this a little later.

2. Beat the whipping cream lightly with a fork and set aside.

3. Put all ingredients except the whipping cream in the bowl of a double boiler over high heat. Begin beating the sauce with a whisk and don't stop until the sauce is thick (about 10 minutes).

4. Once the sauce has thickened, remove the bowl portion of the double boiler (careful, it will be hot!), and place on the pan of cracked ice. Continue beating until the sauce cools down. Once cool, add the lightly beaten cream and whisk until combined. Refrigerate until needed.

The Dinner Date

Marinating the Chefs

This is a hearty, rustic menu, so why not marinate the chefs with a nice imported Italian beer?

Fettucini with Mushroom Sauce

1½ tablespoons olive oil

½ yellow onion

2 cloves garlic (use more, if you like)

Fresh mushrooms (see Dinner Date Hints)

½ ounce dried porcini mushrooms

½ cup chicken broth (or vegetable broth)

¼ cup butter

Fresh basil (10–12 leaves)

Salt (to taste)

Freshly ground pepper (to taste)

Fettucini

Fresh Parmesan cheese

Parmesan Bread

1 loaf Italian bread

¼ cup butter

Freshly grated Parmesan cheese

Dried oregano

Garlic powder (optional)

Tomato and Onion Salad
in an Avocado Shell

1 avocado

1 plum tomato

½ yellow onion

Stealth Dressing

Olive oil

Red wine vinegar

Salt

Freshly ground pepper

1. Remove 1 stick of butter from fridge to let soften for sauce and bread.

2. Finely chop a whole onion. Half will be for the sauce, the other half will be used for the salad.

3. Clean and lightly scrub the mushrooms and chop the ends off the stems. Slice the mushrooms.

4. Place the dried porcini mushrooms in a bowl, and cover with hot water. Set aside.

5. Set a large pot ⅔ filled with water over high heat. This is for the fettucini.

6. Cut 4 to 6 slices of bread and spread out on a cookie sheet. Grate about ¼ cup Parmesan cheese. Butter each slice, then sprinkle each with cheese and oregano. For garlic lovers, sprinkle some garlic powder on each slice. Set aside.

7. Taste the sauce Chef Due has been working on and add more broth, salt, or pepper, if needed. You could also add a splash of white wine if you are feeling creative. Chef Due will ulti-

1. Peel the garlic cloves.

2. In a large sauté pan, heat the olive oil. Using a garlic press, squeeze the garlic in the pan and sauté over medium heat until just golden.

3. When Chef Uno is done chopping the onion, add half of it (the other half is for the salad) at this point (or lower heat until onions are ready). Sauté until they are translucent.

4. Turn the heat down or off under the onion/garlic mixture. And by the way, Chef Uno has a lot of mushrooms to chop. You might want to offer to help.

5. Add the fresh, chopped mushrooms and ½ stick of butter to the onion mixture (don't forget to turn the heat up!) and sauté until the mushrooms are soft.

6. Add the broth, salt, and pepper to the sauce. Let simmer.

7. Using a sharp knife, slice the avocado (with skin on) in half lengthwise. You may have to twist to separate the two halves. Remove the pit by inserting the knife into it and twisting out. Be careful not to cut yourself! You can also use a spoon to dig out the pit, but if the avocado is ripe enough, it should twist out easily enough with the knife. Place the avocado halves on plates.

mately finish the sauce, so here is your chance to make your mark!

8. Coarsely chop the fresh basil for the sauce. Don't add it yet!

9. Check the pot of water. Is it at a rolling boil? If you have bought freshly made fettucini (or made your own), delay this step a bit; but if you are using store-bought fettucini, place it in the boiling water now.

10. Turn on the broiler. When hot, place the Parmesan bread slices under the broiler for about 1 or 2 minutes. Keep an eye on them, you want them to just get slightly crisped.

11. The only thing left to do is to clean the berries. You can save this for after you've eaten or squeeze it in now if the pasta is still cooking.

12. Once the pasta is done, drain and put it in a large bowl. Add the sauce and toss together quickly. Serve with freshly grated Parmesan cheese on top (you can grate it right at the table).

13. Bring the Parmesan bread to the table, and enjoy!

14. Serve the berries later in a bowl with the Sabayon sauce on top.

8. Chop the tomato and add to the chopped onion that Chef Uno so nicely prepared for you. Mix together lightly. Scoop this mixture into the avocado shells letting the extra spill out onto the plate.

9. Make the stealth dressing by pouring olive oil into a bowl or glass for a 4 count (try one-Mississippi, two-Mississippi, etc.). Add vinegar for a 2 count. (Or think about 4 tablespoons of olive oil and 2 of vinegar.) Add a couple of shakes of salt and a couple twists of freshly ground pepper, and mix it all with a fork. Place salad and dressing on the table.

10. Earlier, perhaps without your knowledge, Chef Uno put some dried porcini mushrooms in a bowl of water. They should be nice and soft now, so place a paper towel in a colander or sieve, and drain the mushroom water into another bowl to save. Coarsely chop the porcini mushrooms, and add to your sauce.

11. Add about ¼ cup of the mushroom water and stir well. Increase the heat under your sauce. Stir for about 2 minutes.

12. Taste the sauce one last time, and add the chopped basil. Stir until the basil is well incorporated. Turn heat down until pasta is ready.

13. Open the wine and enjoy!

14. See Chef Uno step 14.

Paella

Sangria

Tomato Bread with Aioli

Seafood Paella

Boston Lettuce Salad

Flan

PREPARATION TIME

About 1$\frac{1}{2}$ hours

Paella was big in America in the sixties and seventies, and no moderately well stocked kitchen was without a paellero, the dish paella is traditionally served in. I remember when I was a kid, during one of my parents' many dinner parties, watching them emerge from the kitchen with a giant shallow bowl filled with this colorful, delicious rice dish. I think eventually the trend gave way to fondue (or was it the other way around?), but it is worth reintroducing paella to our culture because of its ease of preparation, festive quality, and versatility. You never even have to make it the same way twice.

Dinner Date Hints

* You don't have to invest in a paellero, but do make sure you've got a really large, shallow bowl (like a pasta serving bowl) or at least a large skillet for cooking. Traditionally, the dish is placed in the middle of the table, and guests serve themselves. Since there are just two of you, the paella can be served from the kitchen, but I would recommend bringing it to the table because it's such a pretty dish and so very festive.

* Aioli is a garlic mayonnaise that is good on just about everything. In many European countries, it is served at the table as a condiment and is spread or stirred into whatever your heart desires. It may be something you want to make ahead of time and refrigerate so the intensity of the garlic can increase; prepare yourself for a *full* garlic taste. The recipe makes about ½ cup, and you may have leftovers, but if you are a garlic lover like me, the stuff will be gone in a few days. Aioli makes an excellent dip for crudité or hunks of bread.

* A key ingredient for both flavor and color in the paella is saffron. Most grocery stores carry it these days, though you may need to visit a more upscale store. It is a little pricey, but you need only a small amount.

* Feel free to pick and choose what meats go into the paella. Chicken, sausage, shrimp, mussels, and clams are suggested here; you will want to pick about three of those or add something of your own.

❧ The tomato bread can be made with fresh or canned tomatoes. Fresh is preferable, but if there are only sorry-looking tomatoes at your grocery store, go with the canned (and then omit Chef Due step 16).

❧ If you find the sangria too sweet to continue drinking it through dinner, try a nice Spanish red wine. Ask at your local wine store for advice.

❧ Spanish guitar music would be a nice accompaniment to this meal.

Staples

Sugar

Salt

Olive oil

Fresh garlic

Long-grain rice

Vanilla extract

Paprika

Oregano

Produce

3 oranges

3 lemons

1 apple

4 plum tomatoes

1 sweet red pepper

1 sweet green pepper

1 bunch fresh basil

1 yellow onion

1 head Boston lettuce

1 package frozen peas

Dairy and Meat

½ dozen eggs

Butter

Milk

Chorizo, Spanish, or Portuguese
  sausage (optional)

1 chicken breast (optional)

8 clams (optional)

8 shrimp (optional)

8 mussels (optional)

Other

Spanish red wine

½ cup white wine

At least 2 ounces cognac or brandy

1 baguette

Saffron

2 cans chicken broth

Balsamic vinegar

Equipment List

Large, shallow bowl (optional)

Pitcher

Pastry brush

Small soufflé dish or two ramekins

Large cake or broiler pan (for baking
  the flan dish)

Host Prep

If you feel like making the aioli ahead of time (up to two days), follow the directions as outlined in Chef Uno step 5, and Chef Due steps 4 to 9, and then refrigerate until ready. Remember, the earlier you make it, the more intense the garlic flavor!

You need to make the flan at least 2 hours before your date arrives. You can make it the day before if you'll be pressed for time. It only takes about $\frac{1}{2}$ hour to prepare, but the flans must bake for 50 minutes to 1 hour, and then chill for at least 2 hours.

You will need either a small soufflé or casserole dish for the flan, though I prefer to make individual flans in ramekins. Make sure that whatever you use is oven proof! This recipe will make about 4 small flans or 1 larger one. We make the individual ones and eat the leftovers for breakfast. Very decadent, very wonderful!

Flan

¾ cup plus 1 tablespoon sugar

Pinch of salt

1 teaspoon vanilla extract

4 eggs

¼ cup cold milk

2 cups hot milk

1. Preheat the oven to 325°F.

2. Place a small saucepan with 2 cups of milk over low heat. Don't let it boil!

2. In another small saucepan, cook ½ cup of the sugar over medium heat. Stir constantly. When the sugar melts and turns into an amber-colored syrup, pour a spoonful into a ramekin (or pour it all into your single dish, if you are making 1 larger flan). Quickly turn the dish to coat the bottom and as much of the sides as you can. You do have to work quickly as the syrup will harden. Repeat with the remaining ramekins. Set the dish(es) aside.

3. In a medium-sized bowl, combine the last ¼ cup plus 1 tablespoon of sugar, salt, and vanilla. Mix well, and then add the eggs. Stir vigorously until the eggs are well combined (you can use a whisk if you have one).

4. Add the cold milk and stir well. Then add the other milk, which should be hot by now. Mix well.

5. Pour the custard mixture into your caramel coated dish(es). Set the dish(es) in a large cake or broiler pan and put hot water in the pan to cover 1 inch of the flan dish(es).

6. Bake for approximately 1 hour if you've made individual flans, or about 10 or 15 minutes longer if you've made a large single one. You want the custard(s) to look set and not be too jiggly when jostled.

7. Remove from the oven and let cool, still in the pan of water. When completely cool, remove from the pan of water, cover loosely with plastic wrap, and chill in the refrigerator until ready to serve.

8. To serve, carefully run a butter knife around the edge of the flan. Take a dessert or serving plate that is at least 2 inches bigger in diameter than the flan, and place it over the flan dish. Then flip. Either serve the individual flans or slice the larger one into individual portions.

Marinating the Chefs

Make that pitcher of sangria and have a glass or two. If you are going to be drinking the sangria throughout dinner as well, you might want to halve the amount of brandy—they can be quite strong, so be prepared! If you want to go nonalcoholic, try an Orangina (a light orange soda from France) with an extra squeeze of orange in it.

Sangria

1 bottle Spanish red wine

1 shot (or less) cognac or brandy

2 oranges, halved

1 orange, sliced

1 lemon, halved

1 lemon, sliced

1 apple, cubed

Sugar to taste

Aioli

4 garlic cloves

$1/4$ teaspoon salt

2 egg yolks

$3/4$ cup olive oil

1 tablespoon fresh lemon juice

Paella

1 chicken breast

8 shrimp

8 clams

8 mussels

1 chorizo (Spanish or Portuguese sausage)

2 tablespoons olive oil

$\frac{1}{2}$ yellow onion

1 cup long-grain rice

2 cups chicken broth

$\frac{1}{8}$–$\frac{1}{4}$ teaspoon saffron

2 cloves garlic

$\frac{1}{2}$ teaspoon paprika

$\frac{1}{4}$ teaspoon oregano

1 red pepper

1 green pepper

$\frac{1}{2}$ cup white wine

1 bunch fresh basil

$\frac{1}{2}$ package frozen peas

Tomato Bread

1 baguette

1 clove garlic

2 tablespoons olive oil

4 plum tomatoes

Boston Lettuce Salad

1 head Boston lettuce
Balsamic vinegar

1. Preheat the oven to 400°F. This is for the tomato bread and the chicken if you are adding it to the paella.

2. Open the red wine and pour into a large pitcher. Add the cognac and stir.

3. Cut 2 oranges in half and squeeze each half into the wine. Do the same with 1 lemon. Stir well.

4. Add the sliced fruit and about 1 tablespoon of sugar. Stir well. Add several handfuls of ice and stir again. Now it is time to taste. Add sugar if you and Chef Due think it is needed.

5. Separate the egg yolks for the aioli. If you need extra help, please see Helpful Hints.

6. Does Chef Due need a hand? If not, proceed to your next step.

7. If you are adding chicken to the paella, season the breast with salt and pepper, then bake in the preheated oven for about 20 minutes, or until done.

8. If you are adding shrimp, wash, peel, and devein, then set aside.

1. Slice 1 orange and 1 lemon, and set aside 2 particularly pretty orange slices for garnish.

2. Core and then cut the apple into rough cubes.

3. Taste the sangria and tell Chef Uno if you think more sugar is required.

4. Peel five garlic cloves. Two for the aioli, two for the paella, and one for the tomato bread.

5. Using a garlic press, press the garlic into a medium-sized bowl. Add the salt and egg yolk, and beat well with a whisk. Let it sit for 5 minutes.

6. Add a spoonful of olive oil and whisk well.

7. Whisking constantly, add the remaining olive oil a small amount at a time. You can ask Chef Uno to pour the olive oil in a thin stream while you whisk constantly. Or if you're getting tired of whisking, ask Chef Uno to take a turn. Note: This can also be done in a food processor.

8. Once all the oil has been added and the aioli is thick, whisk in the lemon juice. Add more salt to taste.

9. Cover with plastic wrap and refrigerate until ready to serve.

9. If you are adding clams or mussels, scrub well and set aside.

10. If you are adding sausage, remove from the casing and cut into large chunks.

11. Warm the olive oil in a very large skillet or pot. Add the onions Chef Due sliced. Sauté until golden.

12. Add the cup of rice and sauté until lightly browned.

13. Add the warm chicken broth and stir, then add the saffron.

14. Using a garlic press, press the two garlic cloves into the rice mix. (Ask Chef Due for the peeled garlic.) Turn the heat up. Add the paprika and oregano, then the pepper slices when they are ready.

15. Add the sausage (if you are using it), and once the entire mixture boils, turn heat to low and cover.

16. Let it simmer for about 10 minutes. If you are adding clams, add them after approximately 5 minutes.

17. Wash and then coarsely chop the fresh basil.

18. After simmering the paella for 10 minutes, add the white wine, basil, frozen peas, and rest of the meat ingredients you are using. Stir a few more times. Cover and simmer again

10. Thinly slice ½ onion for the paella and set aside.

11. Warm the 2 cups of chicken broth in a small pan over medium heat.

12. Clean, seed, and slice the red and green peppers. Set aside.

13. Mince the garlic clove. In a small bowl, pour a little olive oil and add the garlic.

14. Slice the bread thinly, and with a pastry brush, brush each slice with a little of the olive oil/garlic mixture. Make sure the garlic pieces get distributed on all the bread slices.

15. Place each slice on a cookie sheet covered with foil and put in the oven. I prefer to briefly toast the bread so it is still slightly chewy. Toast it as long as you and Chef Uno agree.

16. While the bread is toasting, take a small saucepan and fill with water. Put the plum tomatoes in and place it over high heat. When the tomato skins begin to crack and peel slightly, remove them and let cool. Check the bread in the oven!

for about 10 minutes until the shrimp is pink and the rice is tender.

19. If you are adding chicken, cut the chicken breast into chunks. Add to the paella about 7 minutes into the final simmer.

20. While waiting for the paella to finish, help Chef Due finish the tomato bread.

21. Once the paella is ready, either bring it to the table and serve yourselves from there, or serve yourselves from the kitchen. Don't forget the flan! ¡Ole!

17. While the tomatoes cool, wash and tear the lettuce. Drain or dry in a salad spinner, then place in a salad bowl. Drizzle a little balsamic vinegar (about 2 tablespoons) on top and toss quickly.

18. Peel the cooled tomatoes. Chop and slightly mash the tomatoes in a bowl.

19. Spread the tomato mash on the toasted bread—chunky is good.

20. Put a small dollop of aioli on each piece of tomato bread.

21. ¡Ole!

Separating an Egg

Have two small bowls nearby. With a knife, or on the side of the bowl, crack the egg over one of the bowls. Keep the egg in one half of the egg shell while keeping the other half of the egg shell in your other hand. Let the egg whites pour out over the egg shell and into the bowl while being careful not to let the egg yolk fall out. Transfer the egg yolk into the empty egg shell half, letting the remaining egg white pour out into the bowl. Repeat until all the egg white has been separated. Drop the egg yolk into the other bowl.

If a little yolk gets into the whites, try to pick it out carefully with a spoon. If that doesn't work, dump the egg white and yolk together into a third bowl and refrigerate for scrambled eggs or for another cooking project later. A little egg yolk in your egg whites could potentially result in great inconvenience; for example, a bit of yolk will cause the egg white not to whip into soft peaks, so don't fudge on this one. If I'm separating a lot of eggs, I like to put out three bowls, one for all the whites, one for all the yolks, and one to hold each egg over one at a time. That way if I screw up I don't ruin all the other egg whites.

Peeling Garlic

Here's a little hint for peeling garlic: With the skin still on the garlic clove, place the flat side of your knife on top of the clove. Hit the flat of the knife with enough force to gently bruise the garlic. This will cause the skin to practically fall off the clove, and minimize your workload.

Roasting Garlic

You'll find that several of my recipes call for roasted garlic. In each of the menus, I suggest that there are two ways to roast a head of garlic: by oven or by microwave. One is slow, the other fast. Both work very well, but I can't help but feel that the slow way results in a milder, better flavor. Take your pick, but if you do have time, try oven roasting.

Roasting garlic in the oven

Preheat oven to 375°F, or if you are cooking something else in the oven at the same time that requires a temperature of 350° or even 400°, go ahead and roast the garlic at the same time. Obviously it will take a little longer in the cooler oven and will be quicker in the hotter. Slice the top (the narrow part) off the head of the garlic, about ½ inch. Place the head in a small baking dish or broiling pan and drizzle a little olive oil over the top of the garlic. Put it in the oven for about 45 minutes, or until the garlic is soft. For a treat while cooking, after the garlic cools slightly, squeeze out a soft clove of the roasted garlic and put on a small slice of buttered French bread. Total heaven.

Roasting garlic in the microwave

Slice the top (the narrow part) off the head of the garlic, about ½ inch. Pierce some of the cloves with a knife, and then drizzle a little olive oil on the top of the garlic. Then wrap the whole head loosely in a paper towel. Put on a microwave-safe plate and microwave on high for about 40 seconds. Turn it over and microwave about 30 seconds. Squeeze it to see if it's soft. Microwave 10 to 20 more seconds if needed.

How to Eat an Artichoke

1. Make sure you have a large, empty bowl on the table to receive the used artichoke leaves. Prepare to get messy! Pull an outer leaf off the head of the artichoke.

2. Put the leaf in your mouth bottom part first and, using your teeth, scrape off the meaty bottom part of the leaf. This should be quite tasty.

3. Continue with the leaves in this manner until you get to the smaller, thinner leaves.

4. Now comes the tricky part: Pull all remaining leaves off the head until you get to the hairy cone or choke (which is nasty), that protects the heart (which is yummy).

5. Using a spoon or table knife, cut the choke away from the heart, until all that hairiness is gone. Be careful not to remove too much of the meat under the hair, this *is* the best part.

6. Eat the artichoke heart, and you are done!

How to Make Homemade Pasta

This recipe makes enough pasta for two people. If you are a huge pasta fan and think that homemade pasta is something you will prepare quite frequently, I suggest you invest in a hand-cranked pasta-cutting machine. Find one that will cut several different widths of pasta: spaghetti, fettucini, lasagna. Avoid the machines that make the dough as well as shape it; you will discover that dough is easy to make yourself, and the machine is not worth the investment.

I sometimes feel that pasta machines were designed for four hands instead of two. If you are going to make homemade pasta for a Dinner Date, please do it together. It is a lot more fun, not to mention easier, when done as a team.

1 cup all-purpose flour

1 large egg

1–3 tablespoons cold water

Making the dough in a food processor

Put the flour, the egg, and 1 tablespoon of water in the bowl of your food processor. Process for about a minute. If the dough does not form into a ball on the top of your blade, add a little more water. If the dough does not form a ball but looks more like tiny pebbles that nevertheless squeeze together, remove from the bowl and form into a ball.

Making the dough by hand

Put the flour in a mixing bowl and make a little well in the center with a wooden spoon. Break the egg into the well and add 1 tablespoon of the water. Stir together until a stiff dough has formed (your hands may work better here than a spoon). Turn the dough out onto a board or countertop and knead until pasta is a smooth ball. Add a little water if the dough is too crumbly.

Forming the dough using a pasta machine

The manufacturer of your machine will have directions, but here are a few things they may not have thought of: Make your dough at least ½ hour before you anticipate rolling it out. Wrap it well in plastic wrap and refrigerate while you clear enough counter space to roll it out (you'll need quite a bit of space!). When you are ready to roll (literally), set up your machine with space on either side. Have all-purpose flour nearby and sprinkle it over your work area. Have a large chopping board or cookie sheet on hand to receive the cut pasta as you cut it in batches.

Remove the pasta dough from the refrigerator and unwrap. Cut it in half and flatten one half with your palm. Rewrap the other half of the dough and put aside. If the dough seems sticky add a little flour and knead it into the dough. If the dough seems dry, add a droplet of water and knead it in.

Pass the flattened half of pasta dough through the smooth rollers set on the widest setting. Fold over and pass this through again. Keep passing the dough through the smooth rollers, gradually lowering the setting to the thinnest or next to thinnest depending on what you prefer. When the piece of pasta gets too long, cut in half and continue with the two pieces.

Once the dough is the thickness you like, pass it through the cutting portion of the machine, catching the cut pasta on the other side. This is where a partner is especially helpful. Place the cut pasta on your board or cookie sheet and sprinkle lightly with flour. As you go along, make sure the already-cut pasta does not stick together; to do this, toss occasionally with a little flour, and run the pasta through your hands. Try to cook the pasta soon after cutting it.

Repeat all of the above with the remaining dough.

Forming the dough by hand

When I was a kid and my family would make homemade pasta (before the mass production of pasta machines), we would hand roll it and cut different shapes. We had a cookie cutter about the size of a grapefruit in the shape of the United States and one time I made noodles with this cookie cutter. Of course, I had to eat the result, which was when I learned that sometimes less is more.

In any case, when forming pasta by hand, it is important to roll it out on a floured surface to uniform thinness. Do this in batches since you will want to roll rectangular pieces to simplify cutting. Once you have achieved your desired thinness, cut the strands of pasta. You can cut it in long strips, or loosely roll up the pasta like a rug and slice. Try for the width of fettucini (about ¼ inch wide) or even pappardelle (¾ inch to 1 inch wide).

Cooking fresh pasta

If you intend to cook the pasta within ½ hour of making it, do so in a pot of boiling water for 2 to 3 minutes. If you need to wait longer and the pasta begins to dry (you may want to spread it out so it doesn't all clump together), cook about a half minute longer. Bear in mind that fresh pasta is not an "al dente" product.

You can make fresh pasta many hours ahead and let dry totally if you like. If you do this, separate the strands and let them air dry. We used to hang pasta off the back of chairs; or you can stick a broom handle between two chairs and let the pasta hang over that to dry. Your house will look like a regular pasta factory!

Glossary

al dente   Pasta cooked so that it retains a somewhat firm texture.

bouquet garni   Several fresh herbs—rosemary, thyme, bay leaves—tied together with twine. Used for flavoring soups and stews.

coarsely chop   To chop an ingredient into large chunks.

cream   To beat and stir an ingredient into a creamy consistency.

devein   To remove the dark vein that runs along the spine of a shrimp. This is done with a knife.

dice   To chop an ingredient into small cubes.

dot   To place small chunks of an ingredient (usually butter) all around the top of a dish, often a casserole, pie, or fruit crisp.

double boiler   A bowl that sits in a pot. These can usually be fabricated by pots and bowls you already have. To cook something in a double boiler is to put the ingredient in the bowl and place it over the pot that has 1 to 3 inches of water in it. This process enables the ingredient to cook (or melt) without being directly exposed to heat.

drizzle   To pour a small amount of a liquid ingredient over another.

fold   A way to incorporate a whipped ingredient (like egg whites or cream) into another set of ingredients. It is different from mere mixing because you want to protect all the air whipped into the folded ingredient. To fold, pour the whipped item over your other ingredients. Then take a rubber spatula and, working against the edge of the bowl, gently overturn the whipped ingredient into the other ingredients with swift motions. Repeat until the whipped ingredient is just incorporated. Be careful not to stir or you will lose some of the air.

garlic press   A device that crushes garlic cloves and presses them through small holes into a chosen receptacle.

kebab-able   Okay, I made this one up. Having the quality suitable for skewering on a kebab.

kebab-ing   The act of making kebabs.

marinate (verb)   1. To let a meat or fish portion sit in a set of ingredients to provide and enhance flavor. 2. To give yourself or your cooking partner a libation that enhances everything.

marinade (noun)   A combined set of ingredients in which meat or fish is soaked.

mince   To finely chop an ingredient into very small pieces.

ramekin   A small, individually sized baking dish.

reconstitute   To add water to a dried ingredient to bring it back to its original shape and texture.

sauté   To cook ingredient(s) in an open pan while constantly keeping the ingredients in motion, either by stirring or by manipulating the pan (like the cooks do on TV).

steamer basket   A bowl-shaped basket with holes designed to sit inside a pot. Most steamer baskets also have legs that allow it to sit above the water in the pot for optimal steaming.

tent   To place a large piece of foil over a baking dish that covers it entirely with ample space between the foods and foil.